D1558070

United States
History
Student Workbook

by
John Napp
Wayne King

AGS®

American Guidance Service, Inc.
Circle Pines, Minnesota 55014-1796
800-328-2560

Table of Contents

Printed in the United States of America

ISBN 0-7854-2529-2

Product Number 93343

A0987

Do You Remember?

Directions: Write the answers to these questions using
complete sentences.

1) How have we gained knowledge of the first inhabitants of North
America?

_____

_____

_____

2) From where did the first inhabitants of North America come? By
what route?

_____

_____

_____

3) The history of the first Americans was not written down. How do
experts explain what is known about these people?

_____

_____

_____

4) What hunting tool of the early Americans has been found?

_____

_____

_____

5) As of the year 18,000 B.C., people were no longer able to walk to
North America. Why?

_____

_____

_____

People of Mesoamerica

Directions: Each sentence below tells about a group of early
Mesoamericans. Write the letter of the sentence after the
correct name at the bottom of the page.

a) The ruins of their temples and pyramids remain as examples of
   some of the finest building in Mesoamerica.

b) These people honored a serpent named Quetzalcoatl.

c) They may have settled in Peru as early as 10,000 B.C.

d) Their military forces were very strong.

e) These people studied space and the planets.

f) These people worked as farmers, weavers, or artisans.

g) It is believed that nomads overtook them in A.D. 1200.

h) They carved in jade and stone.

i) These people studied arithmetic.

j) A hieroglyphic slab written by them is thought to be North
   America's oldest writing.

k) Their main city is now called Mexico City.

l) These people began their civilization in Peru in A.D. 1200.

m) Their main city was Tula.

n) They were good builders, lawmakers, and warriors.

o) These people built many buildings, roads, canals, and bridges.

Olmecs h, j

Mayans a, e, i

Toltecs b, g, m

Aztecs D, f, K, o

Incas C, L, n

Identifying Who Said It

Directions: The statements below might have been made by peoples
in the early Southwest. Decide which civilization the
speaker most likely belonged to. After each statement,
write *H* for Hohokam, *M* for Mogollon, *CA* for Chacoan
Anasazi, *MVA* for Mesa Verde Anasazi, or *KA* for
Kayenta Anasazi.

1) "We planted at the advice of our sun priests." _____

2) "I played sports in the village court." _____

3) "My brother brought water from the reservoir." _____

4) "My father and I helped build many miles of irrigation canals."
_____

5) "Our pit houses were called kivas." _____

6) "Each day we made pottery and weavings." _____

7) "My dress was made from woven cotton." _____

8) "Mother knew the time of year by watching the sun and moon."
_____

9) "My civilization began about 200 B.C." _____

10) "We used to live in a pit house, but now we live aboveground."
_____

11) "When my uncle died, we covered his head with pottery."
_____

12) "Many of my great-grandchildren were Pueblos." _____

13) "Our village has a large court." _____

14) "In the 1300s, my people moved into the Rio Grande area."
_____

15) "In 1130, we moved because of a drought." _____

Adena-Hopewell Details

Directions: Fill in the missing word in each sentence below.

1) The _____ people often built mounds in the shape of animals.

2) The Adena dead were first put in small log _____ .

3) The largest Hopewell settlements never had _____ than 400 people.

4) The earliest known Adena people built burial mounds in the _____ River Valley.

5) Unlike many other peoples, the _____ never built great cities.

6) The Adena dead were put in burial rooms filled with tobacco, pipes, and _____ tablets.

7) Many other groups of people adopted Hopewell _____ and customs.

8) Many Adena burial _____ were more than 300 feet across.

9) The Hopewells were descendents of the _____ .

10) Settlements east of the _____ River traded with the Hopewells.

11) One mound near present-day Hillsboro, Ohio, is built in the shape of a giant _____ .

12) Hopewell mounds were built in the form of human beings, panthers, _____ , and birds.

13) The Hopewell held burials services to _____ their dead.

14) Experts believe that Hopewells spent much time celebrating life, rebirth, and _____ .

15) Unlike those of the Adena, Hopewell mounds were built with great _____ .

Do You Remember?

Directions: Write the answers to these questions using
complete sentences.

1) How did jewels, fine silk, perfumes, and spices get from Asia
to Europe?

_____

_____

_____

2) Why did people want to find a route to the Far East by sea?

_____

_____

_____

3) How did the compass help sailors?

_____

_____

_____

4) Why was the book about Marco Polo's adventures in China
important to explorers?

_____

_____

_____

5) What did Christopher Columbus hope to find when he sailed
from Europe?

_____

_____

_____

Important Facts

Directions: Match each person or place in Column A with a detail
in Column B. Write the letter of each correct answer on
the line.

Column A

Column B

_____ **1)** Jacques Cartier

a) Magellan was killed here

_____ **2)** Ferdinand Magellan

b) conquered the Incas

_____ **3)** Florida

c) America was named for him

_____ **4)** Andes Mountains

d) sailed in 1497

_____ **5)** Juan Ponce de León

e) added to Europe's knowledge of North America

_____ **6)** Philippines

f) looked for the "Fountain of Youth"

_____ **7)** Hernando Cortés

g) Cabot reached it on his first trip

_____ **8)** Giovanni da Verrazano

h) conquered the Aztecs

_____ **9)** Newfoundland

i) gold and silver were shipped from mines here

_____ **10)** Amerigo Vespucci

j) sailed the Pacific Ocean

_____ **11)** Diego De Almagro

k) Aztec king

_____ **12)** Montezuma

l) found water route around South America

_____ **13)** Vasco Núñez de Balboa

m) explored St. Lawrence River

_____ **14)** John Cabot

n) killed Pizarro

_____ **15)** Francisco Pizarro

o) Spanish word for flower

New Colonies Crossword

Across

5) Shore reached in April of 1607

6) Name of company given second charter by King James

9) Clue word carved on a tree on Roanoke Island

11) Written agreement granting power in the name of a country

13) Direction ships sailed from Europe to North America

14) Something people were hoping for in America

Down

1) A fleet of warships

2) Man given a charter by Queen Elizabeth to start a colony

3) Colony named in honor of the king

4) French colony on the St. Lawrence River

7) To take or damage things by force

8) The "Lost Colony"

10) Number of expeditions which Raleigh sent to America

12) Man who asked John White to settle on an island off North Carolina

15) Virgina Dare's grandfather

Do You Remember?

Directions: Write the answers to these questions using
complete sentences.

1) When was the colony of Jamestown started and where was
it located?

_____

_____

_____

2) Why did Jamestown get off to a bad start? List three reasons.

_____

_____

_____

3) Jamestown settlers almost gave up. What happened to change
their minds?

_____

_____

_____

4) What government group formed in Jamestown?

_____

_____

_____

5) What did the Virginia Company do to keep tobacco farmers from
leaving?

_____

_____

_____

Review of the Pilgrims and Puritans

Directions: Write the correct word from the Word Bank to complete
each sentence.

<table>
<tr><td colspan="3">Word Bank</td></tr>
<tr><td>Boston</td><td>Massachusetts</td><td>Puritans</td></tr>
<tr><td>destination</td><td>Mayflower</td><td>religious</td></tr>
<tr><td>investors</td><td>Pilgrims</td><td>Separatists</td></tr>
<tr><td>London</td><td>Plymouth</td><td>shares</td></tr>
<tr><td>majority</td><td>provisions</td><td>stock</td></tr>
</table>

1) The _____ Company granted rights to settle in Virginia.

2) King Charles I took strong measures to keep the _____ under control.

3) The _____ disliked the religious policies of James I, King of England.

4) The Pilgrims received aid from the _____ Company.

5) A _____ company is owned by the people.

6) A _____ is a place where one is going.

7) A _____ is a number greater than half of the total.

8) People who contribute money to a company in hope of making more money
are _____ .

9) A group of Pilgrims onboard a ship wrote the _____ Compact.

10) Pilgrims were also known as _____ .

11) Pilgrims and Puritans were looking for _____ freedom in America.

12) The Puritans landed in _____ , Massachusetts.

13) The supplies needed for a trip or voyage are called _____ .

14) The Puritans obtained a charter in the name of the _____ Bay Colony.

15) Parts of a company purchased by its investors are _____ .

Colonial Life

Directions: Circle the correct word to answer each question.

1) As more Europeans came to America, what did the English become?
   powerful   a minority   angry   slaves   the leaders

2) What plant was used to make dye?
   carrot   potato   spinach   sunflower   indigo

3) Expansion was slowed by concern about American Indians and what else?
   no horses   language barriers   poor traveling conditions   illness   work

4) Which group was not part of the middle class?
   shopkeepers   artisans   farmers   indentured servants   teachers

5) What is another word for "protection?"
   refuse   minority   inferiority   refuge   wealth

6) What way of preserving food did the colonists *not* use?
   smoking   refrigeration   salting   drying   pickling

7) What is a word that means an outbreak of disease?
   illness   fever   epidemic   allergy   flu

8) Long, cold winters and what else made farming difficult in New England?
   very little water   too few people   rocky soil   too many cities   insects

9) What was another name for the middle colonies?
   frontier   prairie   middle lands   bread colonies   wheat land

10) Which was a "money crop" in the southern colonies?
   corn   wheat   rice   barley   soybeans

Meanings in Colonial Trade

Directions: Read each numbered statement. Choose the best
meaning for each underlined word from the box below.
Write the meaning in the space provided after each
sentence.

> - Having to do with
>   the arts
>
> - A set of rules
>
> - The need to complete
>   duties or tasks
>
> - Ability to take care of
>   oneself
>
> - People elected to serve
>   in government

1) Colonists wanted to take <u>responsibility</u> for their own success.

   _____

   _____

2) Great Britain did not want the colonies to feel an <u>independence</u>.

   _____

   _____

3) The <u>cultural</u> life of people in the colonies developed quickly.

   _____

   _____

4) <u>Delegates</u> were in charge of making laws.

   _____

   _____

5) The colonists wanted to be able to set their own <u>regulations</u>.

   _____

   _____

Weighing the Benefits

Directions: Each event during colonial trade listed in the box below
benefited either the colonies or Great Britain. Write each
event under the heading it matches (Colonies or Great
Britain) to show who the event benefited.

- Africa wanted rum made in New England.
- Great Britain passed the Navigation Acts in 1660.
- Africans were captured and brought to America as slaves.
- The British took steps to enforce their laws.
- A tax was added to molasses from the West Indies.
- The West Indies wanted spices from Africa.
- The spirit of independence among the colonists was growing.
- Some British officials in the colonies were paid to look the other way.
- People in America from many different countries were increasing in number.
- The Wool Act was passed in 1699.

COLONIES

_____

_____

_____

_____

_____

_____

_____

GREAT BRITAIN

_____

_____

_____

_____

_____

_____

_____

Do You Remember?

Directions: Write the answers to these questions using
complete sentences.

1) What countries had claims in the Ohio Valley?

_____

_____

_____

2) Why was George Washington first sent to visit the Ohio Valley?

_____

_____

_____

3) What was the purpose of the Albany Congress?

_____

_____

_____

4) What advantages did the British in the Ohio Valley have over
the French?

_____

_____

_____

5) What advantages did the French in the Ohio Valley have?

_____

_____

_____

Details of the French and Indian War

Directions: Match each item in Column A with a detail in
Column B. Write the letter of each correct answer
on the line.

Column A

_____ **1)** William Henry

_____ **2)** King George II

_____ **3)** encouragement

_____ **4)** survivor

_____ **5)** Ohio Valley

_____ **6)** George Washington

_____ **7)** William Pitt

_____ **8)** Crown Point

_____ **9)** Louisbourg

_____ **10)** Edward Braddock

_____ **11)** colonists

_____ **12)** Duquesne

_____ **13)** American Indians

_____ **14)** ambush

_____ **15)** France

Column B

a) prime minister of Great Britain

b) to carry out a surprise attack

c) fort in New York

d) French naval base in Nova Scotia

e) allies of France in the war

f) fought alongside the British

g) suggested ways General Braddock should
prepare for battle at Fort Duquesne

h) words William Pitt offered to the colonists

i) someone who has lived through danger

j) important valley that the British and French
wanted to control

k) surprise attack happened near this fort

l) British monarch

m) had little respect for American Indians as
warriors

n) British lost many men in a failed battle at
this fort

o) joined the American Indians in a war against
the British

A French and Indian War Crossword

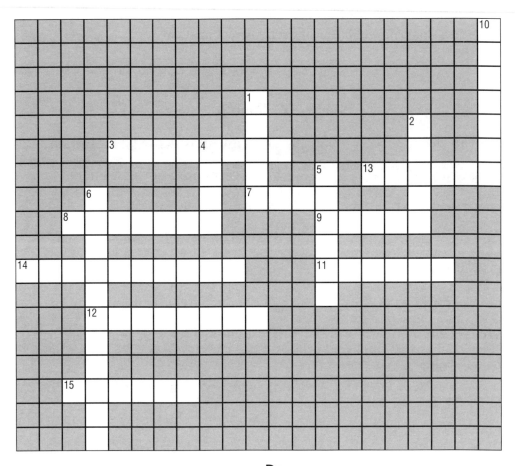

Across

3) French leader at the Battle of Quebec

7) Opposite of west

8) Fort captured by William Johnson and the Iroquois

9) These would be raised to pay for the war

11) Land feature expected to protect Quebec

12) Capture of this fort was a turning point

13) Danger

14) A place well protected from attack

15) General who led several thousand soldiers in 1758

Down

1) British leader who died at Quebec

2) Where the treaty that ended the war was signed

4) Island granted to Spain in exchange for Florida

5) To set upon with violent force

6) New name for French Fort Carillon

10) General who captured Forts Carillon and St. Frederick

Do You Remember?

Directions: Write the answers to these questions using complete sentences.

1) How did Great Britain try to control the American colonies after the French and Indian War ended?

_____

_____

_____

2) Who was Chief Pontiac?

_____

_____

_____

3) Why did Americans think that the Proclamation of 1763 was unfair to them?

_____

_____

_____

4) How did Great Britain set out to raise money after the war?

_____

_____

_____

5) What was the purpose of the Stamp Act?

_____

_____

_____

Colonial Rebellion

Directions: Write the correct word from the Word Bank to complete
each sentence.

Word Bank	
boycotted	repealed
enemy	responsible
finance	soldiers
jobs	taxation
Liberty	troops

1) Great Britain's minister of _____ was
Charles Townshend.

2) Townshend was _____ for a new set of tax laws.

3) Trade slowed down because colonists _____
British goods.

4) Colonists lost _____ in ports where trade
was important.

5) Boston became the center of action against British policies
of _____ .

6) The Sons of _____ took charge of Boston.

7) In order to protect its tax collectors, Britain sent regiments
of _____ .

8) The _____ who fired into the crowd killed
Crispus Attucks.

9) After the Boston Massacre, all of the Townshend taxes were
_____ except for that on tea.

10) The colonists banded together against their common
_____ , the British.

First Continental Congress

Directions: Match each item in Column A with the detail in
Column B. Write the correct letter on the line.

Column A

_____ **1)** Concord

_____ **2)** Samuel Adams

_____ **3)** minutemen

_____ **4)** William Dawes

_____ **5)** John Hancock

_____ **6)** Philadelphia

_____ **7)** Parliament

_____ **8)** Lexington

_____ **9)** General Gage

_____ **10)** Second Continental Congress

_____ **11)** Great Britain's king

_____ **12)** Major Pitcairn

_____ **13)** Samuel Prescott

_____ **14)** John Jay

_____ **15)** Massachusetts

Column B

a) military governor of Massachusetts

b) where First Continental Congress was held

c) was furious about the Declaration of Rights

d) warned colonists British were coming

e) attended the First Continental Congress

f) decided to call a meeting of
colonial representatives

g) would be held if king rejected Declaration
of Rights

h) was sure colonists would have to fight
for freedom

i) where colonists met the British

j) Paul Revere rode through it

k) leader of British regiment

l) warned colonists with Paul Revere

m) where colonists were warned

n) British leaders warned them change was needed

o) soldiers who could gather quickly

Do You Remember?

Directions: Write the answers to these questions using complete sentences.

1) In what ways did the fighting at Lexington and Concord affect the colonists?

_____

_____

_____

2) What did the colonists do to prevent the British from disarming them?

_____

_____

_____

3) What did Ethan Allen and his Green Mountain Boys do to help the colonists?

_____

_____

_____

4) Why was May 10, 1775 an important date in American history?

_____

_____

_____

5) What did some colonists do in an effort to keep the peace?

_____

_____

_____

Complete the Description

Directions: Complete the paragraphs below. Choose the correct term from the Word Bank. Some terms may be used more than once.

Word Bank		
Benjamin Franklin	interfere	protection
control	losses	reorganized
General Gage	loyalty	trading
General Howe	pardons	victory
George Washington	plea	

The Second Continental Congress knew the government had to provide
1) _____ for the colonies against British attack. It could declare war, but it must not
2) _____ in the personal affairs of the people in the colonies.

A colonial army was formed, with **3)** _____ named its commander in chief by a popular vote of Congress. Congress sent out a **4)** _____ to the colonies for troops and money for the war.

Congress set up a colonial post office, naming **5)** _____ as its postmaster. Agents were sent to other countries to ask for help. Ports were reopened to **6)** _____ with any country except for Britain.

7) _____ , the governor of Boston, placed that city under complete
8) _____ of the British army. He offered **9)** _____ to all colonists who were willing to pledge their **10)** _____ to the king.

In order to protect Dorchester Heights from colonial attack, **11)** _____ planned to arm two hills there. The colonials became aware of his plan. The British warships, upon attacking Breed's Hill and Bunker Hill, expected an easy **12)** _____ . After another attack led by **13)** _____ , the British captured the hills. Both sides suffered heavy **14)** _____ .

Just weeks after the Battle of Bunker Hill, George Washington **15)** _____ the colonial troops. The next spring, Americans captured Dorchester Heights.

Name _____ Date _____

People and Places in the War

Directions: Match each item in Column A with a detail in Column
B. Write the letter of each correct answer on the line.

Column A

_____ **1)** document

_____ **2)** loyalists

_____ **3)** Canada

_____ **4)** location

_____ **5)** Massachusetts

_____ **6)** Montreal

_____ **7)** Thomas Jefferson

_____ **8)** Moore's Creek

_____ **9)** Richard Henry Lee

_____ **10)** Benedict Arnold

_____ **11)** Charleston

_____ **12)** Richard Montgomery

_____ **13)** clause

_____ **14)** orator

_____ **15)** Patrick Henry

Column B

a) wrote the Declaration of Independence

b) he was killed at Quebec

c) Americans turned back naval attack here

d) certain section of a document

e) person good at public speaking

f) he was an orator and statesman

g) official paper or piece of writing

h) he was wounded at Quebec

i) one of the Canadian cities colonials planned to capture

j) thought colonies ought to be "free and independent states"

k) Americans had a victory here in February 1776

l) Americans who supported the king of Great Britain

m) where the British were forming an army in 1775

n) Samuel Adams's home colony

o) place where something is positioned

Facts About the War

Directions: Fill in the missing word in each sentence below.

1) George Washington was sure that the British would try to take control of the New York _____ .

2) He moved several _____ soldiers to New York.

3) General William Howe and his _____ reached Staten Island.

4) King George offered one last opportunity for _____ .

5) If the people _____ , they would be pardoned.

6) When Americans were angered, Howe prepared for _____ .

7) Nathan Hale proved himself at New York as he had earlier at _____ .

8) A _____ is held in order to try to capture a fort or city.

9) Hale offered to go into the enemy ranks to get _____ .

10) Hale said, "I only _____ that I have but one life to lose for my country."

11) After being forced beyond New York, the Americans _____ across the Hudson River.

12) In December of 1776, Washington led an attack on _____ , New Jersey.

13) During a _____ , Washington led his troops across the Delaware River.

14) Washington's army defeated a group of soldiers called _____ .

15) The American army defeated three enemy _____ at Princeton.

Identifying Who Said It

Directions: The statements below might have been made by people
during the turning point of the Revolutionary War.
Decide which person may have made each statement.
For George Washington write *W*, for General Howe
write *H*, for Benjamin Franklin write *F*, for George
Rogers Clark write *C*, and for Horatio Gates write *G*.

1) "Governor Henry has called me into service." _____

2) "We must stop Howe's men from taking Philadelphia."
_____

3) "After our victory at Saratoga, the French agreed to answer my
plea." _____

4) "My plan for attacking New York did not work." _____

5) "I can identify any area of the Ohio Valley." _____

6) "We stopped the British at New York for the rest of the war."
_____

7) "General Burgoyne, I accept your surrender." _____

8) "They didn't make it to Philadelphia—we stopped them at
Germantown." _____

9) "I regret that I did not send reinforcements toward New York."
_____

10) "We set up our quarters at Valley Forge." _____

11) "I can't really explain why we're losing the war." _____

12) "I came to Paris to ask for your help." _____

13) "We moved on to capture Cahokia." _____

14) "Yes, we won the battle at Saratoga." _____

15) "Often my troops had to remain unpaid." _____

Victory Crossword

Across

2) Someone who turns against his or her country

6) He was to deliver takeover plans

8) John Paul Jones's ___ is still an example

9) Arnold fought bravely at ___ and Quebec

10) Place where plans were hidden

12) To release from blame by doing something better

13) British warship that John Paul Jones captured

14) He recaptured inland positions of the British

15) To draw in someone

Down

1) The ___ of Paris ended the Revolutionary War

3) He invaded Virginia

4) Land far away from the coast

5) Having fewer troops than the enemy

7) Last name of man who plotted to turn over West Point

11) John Paul Jones became a great ___ hero

Do You Remember?

Directions: Write the answers to these questions using
complete sentences.

1) After the Revolutionary War ended, what task did the new
country face?

_____

_____

_____

2) What action was necessary for settling disputes over
western land?

_____

_____

_____

3) Under the original government of the thirteen states, why was it
difficult for Congress to act?

_____

_____

_____

4) What was wrong with the use of paper money between states?

_____

_____

_____

5) At this point in history, how were disputes between states settled?

_____

_____

_____

The New Start

Directions: Complete the paragraphs below. Choose the correct
term from the Word Bank. Some terms may be used
more than once.

Word Bank		
central	democratic	reason
committee	existed	states
compromise	justice	system
control	key	Virginia
deadlock	population	

When the delegates met at the Constitutional Convention, they knew that a different
1) _____ of government was needed. Edmund Randolph offered a plan that included
a stronger **2)** _____ government. Larger states would have greater
3) _____ . Known as the **4)** _____ Plan, or the "large state plan," it said
that a state's number of representatives would be based on its **5)** _____ . The
government would have a law-making congress, an enforcement branch, and a court to
guarantee **6)** _____ . Randolph believed that his plan was very **7)** _____ .

New Jersey's William Paterson offered a government plan similar to the one that already
8) _____ . According to his plan, the **9)** _____ would have more control,
and each one would have an equal vote. The delegates disagreed, and it became very clear that a
10) _____ was necessary.

Benjamin Franklin calmed the delegates with his strong sense of **11)** _____ .
However, the smaller and larger states remained in a **12)** _____ . At the heart of their
disagreement was the **13)** _____ issue of whether the states or the federal government
would have more power. A special **14)** _____ was formed to try to work out a
15) _____ .

Constitutional Compromise

Directions: Under each heading below, complete the sentences to give details that tell more about that heading.

1) The Legislative Branch of the Government

   a) This branch would have two houses—

_____

   b) The number of representatives from a state

_____

2) The Judicial Branch of the Government

   a) The highest court in the country would be the

_____

   b) This branch would

_____

3) The Executive Branch of the Government

   a) This branch would be headed by

_____

   b) It would be responsible for

_____

4) Compromises Worked Out in 1787

   a) Three out of five slaves

_____

   b) Until the year 1808, Congress

_____

5) The Northwest Ordinance

   a) The area covered by this ordinance was

_____

   b) As soon as the population of the area became large enough,

_____

Constitutional Match-Up

Directions: Match each item in Column A with a detail in Column B.
Write the letter of each correct answer on the line.

Column A

_____ **1)** Massachusetts

_____ **2)** John Marshall

_____ **3)** ratify

_____ **4)** New Hampshire

_____ **5)** Rhode Island

_____ **6)** Alexander Hamilton

_____ **7)** unanimous

_____ **8)** circulate

_____ **9)** Delaware

_____ **10)** George Washington

_____ **11)** amendment

_____ **12)** *Federalist Papers*

_____ **13)** Patrick Henry

_____ **14)** New York

_____ **15)** John Adams

Column B

a) led the New York Federalists

b) to approve something

c) to pass something among people or places

d) first state to approve the Constitution

e) Coleader of the Anti-Federalists in Virginia

f) John Hancock's state

g) Vice President under George Washington

h) one of the last two states to approve Constitution

i) Coleader of Federalists at the Virginia convention

j) this state's approval decided the vote

k) when all sides agree

l) eleventh state to approve Constitution

m) his offer to serve as President boosted support for Constitution

n) a series of essays

o) a change

Do You Remember?

Directions: Write the answers to these questions using
complete sentences.

1) Who did George Washington choose to be his advisers?

_____

_____

_____

2) At the end of the Revolutionary War, what was the condition of
the treasury?

_____

_____

_____

3) How did Congress respond to Hamilton's financial plan?

_____

_____

_____

4) Why was the capital moved from New York to
Washington, D.C.?

_____

_____

_____

5) What were some of the results of Hamilton's financial plan?

_____

_____

_____

Government's Progress

Directions: Write the correct word or phrase from the Word Bank to complete each sentence.

Word Bank	
American Indians	Federalist party
arguments	Florida
debt	George Washington
Democratic-Republicans	neutral
European	treaty

1) Those who favored Hamilton's ideas made up the _____ .

2) The _____ supported stronger state government.

3) _____ believed that opposing political parties would lead to further disagreement.

4) The United States could not go to war again because it was so far in _____ .

5) When France and Great Britain went to war, President Washington decided the United States should remain _____ .

6) Great Britain had been selling weapons to _____ .

7) John Jay went to London to discuss a _____ .

8) Spain opened the port of New Orleans and it gave the United States a section of _____ .

9) Washington could not decide how to deal with increasing _____ about how the government should be run.

10) Washington kept the nation out of _____ wars.

Adams Administration Crossword

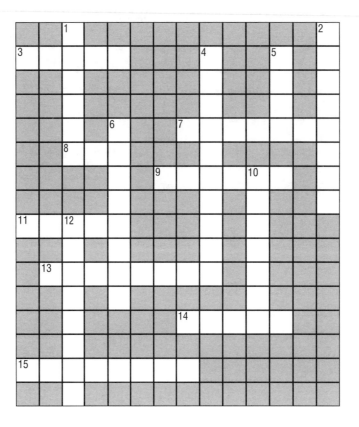

Across

3) The Constitution provides for freedom of speech and freedom of the ___

7) Adams supported the power of the ___ government

8) Vote result in election of 1800

9) X, Y, and Z were agents of this country

11) The states placed a ___ on the national government

13) Showing a feeling of being better than others

14) Someone who lives in one country but is a citizen of another

15) Man who got sixty-four votes in 1800

Down

1) To send someone away from a country

2) Man who influenced Congress about presidential choice

4) Adams's political party

5) Person who got same number of votes as Jefferson

6) Act which made it a crime to speak out against the government

10) Members of the electoral ___ choose the President

12) France agreed not to interfere with American ___ ships

The Louisiana Purchase

Directions: Match each item in Column A with a detail in Column B.
Write the letter of each correct answer on the line.

Column A

_____ **1)** Napoleon Bonaparte

_____ **2)** France

_____ **3)** New Orleans

_____ **4)** Robert Livingston

_____ **5)** West Point

_____ **6)** James Monroe

_____ **7)** Virginia

_____ **8)** Thomas Jefferson

_____ **9)** Minnesota

_____ **10)** Mississippi River

_____ **11)** District of Columbia

_____ **12)** Florida

_____ **13)** Spain

_____ **14)** John Marshall

_____ **15)** Congress

Column B

a) present-day state that was part of Louisiana Purchase

b) where Jefferson was inaugurated

c) forced to surrender Louisiana

d) Chief Justice of Supreme Court

e) country from which America bought Louisiana Territory

f) French leader

g) important port for international trade

h) American ambassador

i) sent to Paris by Jefferson

j) believed Constitution controlled government

k) approved the Louisiana Purchase

l) waterway gained by Louisiana Purchase

m) Jefferson's home state

n) part of $10 million purchase

o) site of United States Military Academy

Growth and Exploration True or False

Directions: Read each sentence. Write *T* if the statement is true or *F*
if it is false.

_____ **1)** President Jefferson sent Lewis and Clark to explore the northwest.

_____ **2)** Lewis and Clark started their journey at Chicago.

_____ **3)** Lewis and Clark reached the Atlantic Ocean.

_____ **4)** From Lewis and Clark's exploration, America learned about the Oregon Country.

_____ **5)** Lewis and Clark claimed the Oregon Country for America.

_____ **6)** Zebulon Pike looked for the source of the Missouri River.

_____ **7)** After following the Arkansas River into the Rockies, Pike reached Pikes Peak.

_____ **8)** Pike was jailed for a while by the French.

_____ **9)** Both France and Great Britain were upset that America was trading with its enemy.

_____ **10)** France set up a trade blockade, while Great Britain did not.

_____ **11)** Jefferson believed that the oceans were neutral.

_____ **12)** France and Great Britain could easily get along without supplies from America.

_____ **13)** With the Embargo Act, Jefferson was seeking to show the world that methods other than war could solve problems.

_____ **14)** American merchants did not like the Embargo Act.

_____ **15)** Jefferson was pleased with the success of the Embargo Act.

Do You Remember?

Directions: Write the answers to these questions using
complete sentences.

1) What new policy did Madison propose?

_____

_____

_____

2) How would Britain be affected if Americans closed ports to the
British?

_____

_____

_____

3) What did the "War Hawks" of the Twelfth Congress want?

_____

_____

_____

4) What ongoing problem did American merchant ships face?

_____

_____

_____

5) What was the difference between America's relationship with
Great Britain and America's relationship with France?

_____

_____

_____

Fill in the Blanks About the New War

Directions: Write the correct word from the Word Bank to complete
each sentence.

Word Bank	
action	industries
defeated	interfered
doubled	organize
established	standstill
frontier	support

1) When James Madison became President, twenty years had
   passed since the Constitution _____ the
   new government.

2) By 1810, the area of the United States had _____
   in size.

3) While the southern states were producing cash crops, the New
   England states were developing _____ .

4) The _____ was being pushed farther west.

5) The War Hawks believed it was time for Americans to
   take _____ .

6) Henry Clay and John C. Calhoun thought Canada could easily
   be _____ .

7) The British had seized American ships and _____
   with trade.

8) Tecumseh tried to _____ a confederacy
   against settlers.

9) America had no money to _____ a
   well-trained army.

10) Foreign trade had almost come to a complete _____ .

During or After

Directions: Write each phrase from the box beneath a heading below the box. Choose the heading that matches the time period of the phrase.

- support was mixed
- westward expansion was safe
- spending was increased
- a battle at New Orleans was fought
- movement of American Indians was forced
- the need to be self-sufficient grew
- everything was in a state of confusion
- Americans met with British in Belgium
- Jackson's popularity spread
- America had a new sense of nationalism

During the War of 1812

_____

_____

_____

_____

_____

_____

_____

After the Treaty of Ghent

_____

_____

_____

_____

_____

_____

_____

Do You Remember?

Directions: Write the answers to these questions using
complete sentences.

1) What helped James Monroe to become elected?

_____

_____

_____

2) From 1790 to 1820, how did the population on the
frontier change?

_____

_____

_____

3) What effect did the Erie Canal have?

_____

_____

_____

4) What were four important problems that westerners faced?

_____

_____

_____

5) How did the invention of the cotton gin affect the South?

_____

_____

_____

Monroe's Era Crossword

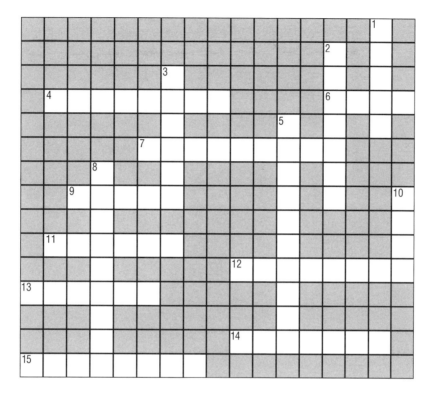

Across

4) Admission of this state caused new slavery debate

6) Speaker of the House

7) Some believe William Plumer wanted George Washington to remain the only President to be elected by a ___ vote

9) Freed slave who had planned to attack South Carolina cities

11) Crop grown in the South

12) American Indians from Florida

13) Rebellion

14) To put to death

15) "Era of Good ___"

Down

1) Present-day state once held by Spain

2) He led an invasion into Spanish Florida

3) Secretary of State Adams's middle name

5) The issue of free states and slave states was settled by the Missouri ___

8) Related to the interests of a region

10) States that weren't slave states were called ___ states

Identifying Who Said It

Directions: The statements below might have been made by famous
people during the early 1800s. Decide who may have
made each statement. For Thomas Jefferson write *TJ*, for
Andrew Jackson write *AJ*, for James Monroe write *JM*,
for John Q. Adams write *JQA*, for George Canning write
GC, and for Henry Clay write *HC*.

1) "I am certain that my military successes will help me win the
election." _____

2) "I encourage an agreement between my country and America."
_____

3) "I know that Clay's efforts kept me out of office." _____

4) "Do I have experience? Why, I have been Speaker of the House."
_____

5) "European countries caused serious problems during my
presidency." _____

6) "Yes, Mr. President, I agree with the British foreign secretary."
_____

7) "A joint declaration is a bad idea." _____

8) "Great Britain has a proposal for us, gentlemen." _____

9) "May I remind you that my father was President." _____

10) "Kentuckians thank you for nominating one of their own."
_____

11) "We must all support Adams." _____

12) "I will win in the next election." _____

13) "I am very upset with the Americans." _____

14) "I have announced the doctrine to Congress." _____

15) "The Monroe Doctrine would have been stronger if our country
had taken part in it." _____

Do You Remember?

Directions: Write the answers to these questions using
complete sentences.

1) Why was John Quincy Adams not a popular President?

_____

_____

_____

2) Which region of the country did not like the tariff system? Why?

_____

_____

_____

3) What three things happened after the Tariff Bill of 1828 was passed?

_____

_____

_____

4) What is meant by the spoils system?

_____

_____

_____

5) What did Jackson consider to be his duty as President?

_____

_____

_____

Southern Tension

Directions: Write the correct word from the Word Bank to complete
each sentence.

Word Bank		
challenge	lowered	oppression
fearful	nullified	revolt
followers	opposed	worship
heritage		

1) Nat Turner and a group of _____ killed slave owners
   and their families.

2) As a result of their _____ , Turner and about twenty
   others were hanged.

3) More than 100 innocent Africans were killed by
   _____ masters.

4) Slaves gained a new courage to fight _____ .

5) The South and West _____ the tariff act passed
   under President Adams.

6) Enslaved Africans had to _____ in the fields as they
   worked.

7) Much American folk song _____ comes from
   African Americans.

8) A new tariff act passed in 1832 _____ some tariffs.

9) South Carolina passed an ordinance that _____
   tariffs in their state.

10) President Jackson felt that no state should be allowed to
    _____ the country's unity.

Facts About Texan Independence

Directions: Match each item in Column A with a detail in Column
B. Write the letter of each correct answer on the line.

Column A

_____ **1)** John Quincy Adams

_____ **2)** Mexico

_____ **3)** William Travis

_____ **4)** Jim Bowie

_____ **5)** Antonio López de Santa Anna

_____ **6)** Alamo

_____ **7)** Goliad

_____ **8)** San Jacinto

_____ **9)** Sam Houston

_____ **10)** Texas

_____ **11)** President Jackson

_____ **12)** Santa Fe

_____ **13)** Louisiana

_____ **14)** Texans

_____ **15)** San Antonio

Column B

a) river near the Gulf of Mexico

b) offered Mexico $5 million for Texas

c) commander of Texas army

d) would not sell Texas

e) town near Alamo

f) refused to obey Mexican laws

g) state east of Texas

h) offered Mexico $1 million for Texas

i) Mexican dictator

j) town that was part of the land claimed by
Texas and Mexico

k) Texan colonel

l) town in south Texas where Santa Anna
won battle

m) rebuilt mission

n) famous westerner who died at Alamo

o) Houston became its president

Election of 1836

Directions: Complete the paragraphs below. Choose the correct
phrase from the Word Bank.

Word Bank	
become careless	manufacturers and shippers
central government	road and canals
entered a depression	rushed to banks
factories and mills	same approach
farm products	the national bank charter
given loans	three Whig candidates
gold or silver	unemployment spread
manufactured goods	

    In the election of 1836, Whig candidates Henry Clay and Daniel Webster received strong
support from northeastern **1)** _____ . These men promoted the renewal of
2) _____ , high tariffs, and a strong **3)** _____ . Martin Van Buren wanted
people to know that a vote for him was like a vote for Jackson, because he believed in the
4) _____ . Van Buren got more votes than the **5)** _____ all together.

    Shortly after President Van Buren took office, the country **6)** _____ , called the
Panic of 1837. A good number of Jackson's smaller banks had **7)** _____ . Paper money
was not backed up by **8)** _____ . Some had **9)** _____ that were never paid
back. When word of these problems got out, many people **10)** _____ to take out
money deposited earlier.

    As a result of the panic, many **11)** _____ closed. Prices fell on
12) _____ and **13)** _____ . New construction of **14)** _____
stopped. During this depression, which lasted several years, **15)** _____ .

Do You Remember?

Directions: Write the answers to these questions using
complete sentences.

1) Between 1790 and 1840, what percentage of Americans lived in cities?

_____

_____

_____

2) Why were bankers not eager to lend money to manufacturers?

_____

_____

_____

3) What advantage did the steel plow offer over wooden plows?

_____

_____

_____

4) Who provided financial support to Samuel Slater in Rhode Island?

_____

_____

_____

5) What was used as fuel in the making of iron?

_____

_____

_____

Transportation and Communication Crossword

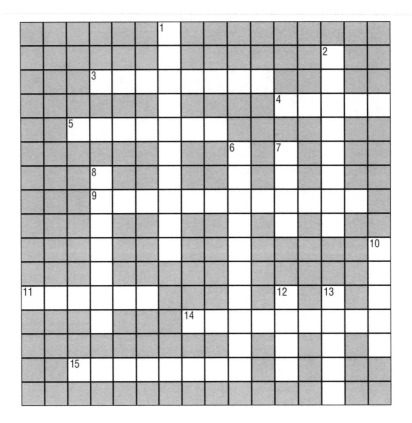

Across

3) Buying or selling goods

4) Man who laid underwater cable

5) The pony _____ carried mail

9) Rail cars brought boats over these mountains

11) Inventor of steam-powered boat

14) Most important improvement in transportation

15) A road travelers pay to use

Down

1) 600-mile road to the West

2) Name of first steam-powered boat

6) Engine that rides on rails

7) To transport goods

8) Robbers

10) He developed the telegraph

12) Lake near New York City

13) Human-made waterway

Immigrant Facts

Directions: In the box are facts about immigrants from Ireland and Germany. Write each fact under the correct heading below. Some facts may apply to either group of immigrants.

> • by 1850, nearly one and a half million of them lived in America
>
> • left their homeland due to a potato failure
>
> • by 1850, about four million of them lived in America
>
> • they had escaped political problems in their homeland
>
> • they became a part of the American melting pot
>
> • many of these people came to America between 1790 and 1820
>
> • they depended on potatoes for food in their homeland
>
> • they faced hunger in their homeland
>
> • they hoped for a better life in America
>
> • they had no choice but to leave their homeland

Germans

_____

_____

_____

_____

_____

_____

_____

_____

Irish

_____

_____

_____

_____

_____

_____

_____

_____

Early Education

Directions: Write the correct word from the Word Bank to complete each sentence.

Word Bank		
academies	Public	taxes
democracy	reference book	tutors
education	standard	vote
grammar		

1) Many wealthy families paid _____ to teach their children.

2) Some older children attended _____ and colleges.

3) _____ education was not a popular idea, especially with working-class families.

4) People began to realize that education was important so people could _____ wisely.

5) Thomas Jefferson had said _____ calls for an educated people.

6) In Massachusetts, schools were supported by state _____ .

7) Noah Webster wrote a series of readers, spellers, and _____ books.

8) A _____ is a book used to find information.

9) Horace Mann was in charge of _____ for the state of Massachusetts.

10) Webster's books provided a _____ of learning for American schoolchildren.

Identifying Who Said It

Directions: The statements below might have been made by famous
people during the 1800s. Decide who may have made
each statement. For Henry Wadsworth Longfellow write
HWL, for Edgar Allan Poe write *EAP*, for John James
Audubon write *JJA*, for Harriet Beecher Stowe write
HBS, for Frederick Douglass write *FD*, and for James
Fenimore Cooper write *JFC*.

1) "Oh, yes, I will give a speech, if that will help people realize the evils of slavery." _____

2) "The country would run best under the guidance of a few successful people." _____

3) "Could I interest you in a copy of *The North Star*?" _____

4) "I like to think that my book helped end slavery." _____

5) "I want to help people find out the news of the country." _____

6) "I have scared them out of their wits." _____

7) "When it comes to drawing, I must say that birds are my specialty." _____

8) "Yes, I am from New England. Does that mean I can't be concerned about the South?"
_____

9) "It pleases me that you like Leatherstocking." _____

10) "Of course, my most famous poem may be "The Raven." _____

11) "If you are interested in the French and Indian War, I have written something for you."
_____

12) "I never went to school—I taught myself all I need to know." _____

13) "Bill MacGillivray and I work well together." _____

14) "Thousands of copies of my book were sold after it was released in 1852." _____

15) "My poem gives readers a look at that famous ride at the beginning of the Revolutionary
War." _____

Do You Remember?

Directions: Write the answers to these questions using
complete sentences.

1) Who were the presidential candidates in the election of 1840? Which party did each
candidate represent?

_____

_____

_____

2) Why was William Henry Harrison so well known?

_____

_____

_____

3) What were some of the new election ideas tried by the Whigs?

_____

_____

_____

4) Why did President Tyler have problems with Congress?

_____

_____

_____

5) How was the problem with Maine settled?

_____

_____

_____

People and Places

Directions: Match each item in Column A with a detail in Column
B. Write the letter of each correct answer on the line.

Column A

_____ **1)** Guadalupe Hidalgo

_____ **2)** Rio Grande

_____ **3)** Zachary Taylor

_____ **4)** James Polk

_____ **5)** Nueces

_____ **6)** Nicholas Trist

_____ **7)** Winfield Scott

_____ **8)** John Slidell

_____ **9)** Stephen Kearny

_____ **10)** California

_____ **11)** Mexico City

_____ **12)** Sam Houston

_____ **13)** Texas

_____ **14)** Santa Anna

_____ **15)** United States

Column B

a) river Taylor advanced beyond

b) "Old Fuss and Feathers"

c) as of 1848, it stretched from coast to coast

d) United States offered $25 million for it

e) boundary between Texas and Mexico

f) he had surrendered to Houston

g) was sent to Mexico City

h) he led the first battle of the Mexican War

i) President during Mexican War

j) treaty that ended the Mexican War

k) American leader in Texas War of Independence in 1836

l) one of the American leaders who invaded California

m) he negotiated the Treaty of Guadalupe Hidalgo

n) where offer to purchase California was presented

o) joined the Union in 1845

Do You Remember?

Directions: Write the answers to these questions using
complete sentences.

1) How many free states and slave states were there in 1848?

_____

_____

_____

2) How long did Zachary Taylor serve as President?

_____

_____

_____

3) How did the Compromise of 1850 affect slavery in the District of Columbia?

_____

_____

_____

4) What law made it easier for slave owners to recapture runaway slaves?

_____

_____

_____

5) What state did the U.S. government pay $10 million to give up its claim to New Mexico?

_____

_____

_____

Slavery Issues Crossword

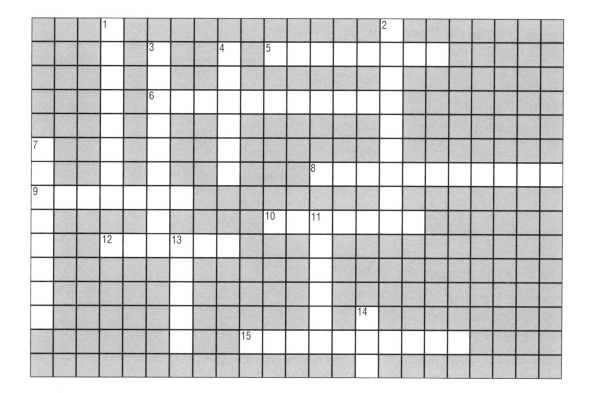

Across

5) Locations on freedom route

6) The _____ Railroad helped slaves escape

8) _____ did not think slavery was wrong

9) Man who worked out the purchase of land in 1853

10) System linked together in some way

12) Important crop in the South

15) Large farm on which crops such as tobacco, sugar, or cotton are grown

Down

1) Former slave who helped free others

2) Name for a person who worked the Underground Railroad

3) Now New Mexico and Arizona

4) President in 1853

7) Running from the law

11) Harriet _____ spoke out against slavery

13) Sojourner _____ also spoke out against slavery

14) Cotton was an important _____ material for northern textile industries

The 1850s

Directions: Complete the paragraphs below. Choose the correct
term from the Word Bank.

Word Bank		
connected	northern	slavery
conflicts	population	sovereignty
covered	produce	tension
Fugitive	routes	territory
introduced	ship	travel

Since the time it joined the Union, the **1)** _____ of California had grown a
good deal. Thousands of people traveled to the West by **2)** _____ wagon in a very
long journey.

The railroads **3)** _____ cities throughout the East. Businesses used them to
4) _____ their goods. Farmers were able to bring their **5)** _____ to market
by railroad. People could **6)** _____ more safely than ever before. Congress discussed
possible **7)** _____ for a coast-to-coast railroad, but the members could not agree.

Northerners had to deal with the problem of building a railroad through Nebraska, which
was not a **8)** _____ . Stephen Douglas **9)** _____ a bill to allow Nebraska to
become a territory. In a plan called popular **10)** _____ , the residents of the states
would have the choice to enter the Union as slave states or free states.

Passage of the Kansas-Nebraska Act caused many **11)** _____ among political
parties. The slavery issue had been a greater problem as **12)** _____ between slave
states and free states continued to grow.

In 1854, Democrats, Free Soilers, and **13)** _____ Whigs met and formed the
Republican party. This new party wanted to take a clear stand on **14)** _____ . The
party wanted to repeal the **15)** _____ Slave Law and the Kansas-Nebraska Act.

Do You Remember?

Directions: Write the answers to these questions using
complete sentences.

1) Most of the proslavery settlers who moved to Kansas came from which southern states?

_____

_____

_____

2) The violence between the proslavery and the antislavery groups in the Kansas territory led to what nickname for the area?

_____

_____

_____

3) Who was John Brown?

_____

_____

_____

4) Which senator led the proslavery group in Kansas? Which state did he represent?

_____

_____

_____

5) What was the estimate of property damage caused by the violence in Kansas in 1856?

_____

_____

_____

The Late 1850s

Directions: Read each statement. Decide whether it applies to
Abraham Lincoln, Stephen Douglas, John Brown, or
Robert E. Lee. On the line next to the statement, write
Lincoln, Douglas, Brown, or *Lee.*

_____ 1) This man was barely over five feet tall.

_____ 2) His men captured John Brown.

_____ 3) For two years, he had been a member of the House of Representatives.

_____ 4) His crime was treason.

_____ 5) People considered him an excellent speaker.

_____ 6) He debated with Stephen Douglas.

_____ 7) He believed that violence was sometimes necessary.

_____ 8) Charlestown, Virginia, was the place of his death.

_____ 9) He was not a strong public speaker.

_____ 10) This debater knew he had made a mistake.

_____ 11) Slaves, he believed, should be armed against their masters.

_____ 12) This colonel was sent to Virginia with marines.

_____ 13) The capture of Harper's Ferry was his success.

_____ 14) People began to call him "Honest Abe."

_____ 15) He lost the Senate election.

The Election of 1860

Directions: The phrases in the box were true of northern Democrats, southern Democrats, Republicans, or the Constitutional Union party. Write each phrase under the correct heading below.

- believed that peace required cooperation
- nominated Stephen Douglas
- believed in higher tariffs
- received eighteen percent of the vote
- won the election
- nominated John Bell
- said slave states could make decisions about slavery within their own borders
- supported popular sovereignty

- supported slavery
- nominated Abraham Lincoln
- nominated John Breckinridge
- territories could offer free land for farming
- made up of former American party members and Whigs
- received twenty-nine percent of the vote
- received thirteen percent of the vote

Northern Democrats

_____

_____

_____

_____

_____

Southern Democrats

_____

_____

_____

_____

_____

Republicans

_____

_____

_____

_____

Constitutional Union

_____

_____

_____

_____

Do You Remember?

Directions: Write the answers to these questions using complete sentences.

1) What plan did President Buchanan have to bring the country back together again?

_____

_____

_____

2) What compromise did Senator John Crittenden suggest for preserving the Union?

_____

_____

_____

3) How did the southern states go about forming their own government?

_____

_____

_____

4) How did President Buchanan respond to the Fort Sumter situation?

_____

_____

_____

5) What challenges faced President Lincoln when he took office?

_____

_____

_____

From Fort Sumter Onward

Directions: Match each item in Column A with a detail in Column
B. Write the letter of each correct answer on the line.

Column A

_____ **1)** General Beauregard

_____ **2)** Richmond

_____ **3)** Robert E. Lee

_____ **4)** The North

_____ **5)** Mississippi River

_____ **6)** Abraham Lincoln

_____ **7)** General Winfield Scott

_____ **8)** Robert Anderson

_____ **9)** Anaconda Plan

_____ **10)** Jefferson Davis

_____ **11)** Southerners

_____ **12)** Virginia

_____ **13)** Fort Sumter

_____ **14)** Confederacy

_____ **15)** South Carolina

Column B

a) "Old Fuss and Feathers"

b) had eleven states

c) Scott's plan for winning the war

d) were fighting for land and rights

e) Union major at Fort Sumter

f) South Carolina Confederate commander

g) new Confederate capital

h) site of solid Confederate defense

i) Confederate general

j) Scott had all shipping here stopped

k) ordered blockade of seceded states

l) had most of the factories

m) location of Fort Sumter

n) Confederate President

o) fort where first battle occurred

Civil War Crossword

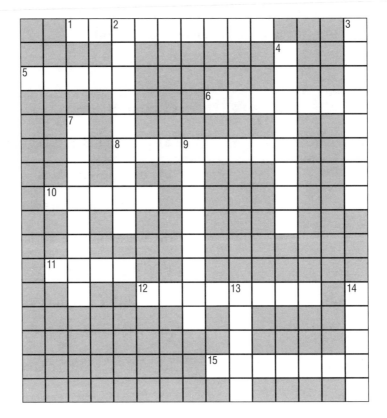

Across

1) Thomas J. Jackson's nickname

5) He was replaced by McClellan

6) McClellan led the Union army of the _____

8) It was renamed *Virginia*

10) Antietam _____

11) Battle of _____ Run

12) Battle was fought here in August of 1862

15) Experienced or former member of the armed forces

Down

2) To have more people than an opponent in a battle

3) In March of 1862, Confederates wanted to break the northern _____

4) Ship with iron-plated sides

7) Under his control, the Union gained most of the Mississippi Valley

9) Confederate capital

13) Number of Days Battles

14) He led the capture of Fort Henry

The Continuing War

Directions: The statements in the box could be said of people in the Union or the Confederacy. Write each statement under the correct heading at the bottom of the page.

- They did not think Lincoln would free all the enslaved people.
- George Pickett led 13,000 men toward the line at Gettysburg.
- Joseph Hooker led them at Chancellorsville.
- They won at Gettysburg.
- Originally they had planned a defensive war.
- A small army remained at Fredericksburg.
- George Meade led 85,000 men at Gettysburg.
- Their leader thought a major northern victory would end the war.

- 180,000 formerly enslaved people joined its army.
- Lee retreated to the Potomac River.
- Their victory at Antietam had been important.
- Stonewall Jackson was wounded by his own men.
- Twenty-three African soldiers won the Medal of Honor.
- Lee approached Pennsylvania with 65,000 men.
- Their leader thought of trying to win back the West.

Union

_____

_____

_____

_____

_____

_____

_____

_____

_____

Confederacy

_____

_____

_____

_____

_____

_____

_____

_____

_____

Do You Remember?

Directions: Write the answers to these questions using
complete sentences.

1) Under President Lincoln's plan, how could a state rejoin the Union?

_____

_____

_____

2) Who shot President Lincoln? Why did he shoot Lincoln?

_____

_____

_____

3) What were three problems that faced the southern states after the Civil War?

_____

_____

_____

4) What was a problem for President Johnson in dealing with Congress?

_____

_____

_____

5) What were the "Black Codes?"

_____

_____

_____

Rebuilding the South

Directions: Match each item in Column A with a detail in Column
B. Write the letter of each correct answer on the line.

Column A

_____ **1)** Tenure of Office Act

_____ **2)** William Seward

_____ **3)** southern whites

_____ **4)** American Indians

_____ **5)** Edwin Stanton

_____ **6)** Senate

_____ **7)** African Americans

_____ **8)** Radical Republicans

_____ **9)** House of Representatives

_____ **10)** Tennessee

_____ **11)** Civil Rights Act of 1866

_____ **12)** Freedmen's Bureau

_____ **13)** Ulysses S. Grant

_____ **14)** Horatio Seymour

_____ **15)** Reconstruction Act of 1867

Column B

a) 450,000 voted for Grant

b) only Confederate state that immediately
accepted the Fourteenth Amendment

c) won in a very close popular vote

d) voted to impeach Johnson

e) was meant to reverse "Black Codes"

f) blamed Republicans for the Civil War

g) put ten states under military rule

h) was vetoed by Johnson

i) held a trial to make final impeachment
ruling

j) arranged the purchase of Alaska

k) fired by President Johnson

l) lost election to Grant

m) were not covered by Fourteenth
Amendment

n) got many bills passed in Congress

o) formed to help formerly enslaved people

End of Reconstruction

Directions: Complete the paragraphs below. Choose the correct term from the Word Bank.

Word Bank		
carpetbaggers	murder	scalawags
clauses	outcome	scandals
conditions	prevented	suffrage
depression	Reconstruction	taxes
equality	rich	troops

The Fifteenth Amendment guaranteed **1)** _____ to all male Americans except for American Indians. Southerners became concerned because they feared that African Americans would be able to decide the **2)** _____ of an election. In some states, African Americans were **3)** _____ from voting. Some states passed laws with grandfather **4)** _____ that made many African Americans ineligible to vote.

The Ku Klux Klan wanted to make **5)** _____ leave the South and to punish the **6)** _____ . Often the violence of the Klan, while intended to scare their victims, led to **7)** _____ .

President Grant's administration was harmed by many **8)** _____ . Many of the friends he appointed to government positions tried to get **9)** _____ through their power in government. During Grant's second term in office, the country went into a **10)** _____ .

After ten years of the Reconstruction, northerners grew tired of it. They disliked the high **11)** _____ , and they felt it was time for the South to take care of itself. Rutherford B. Hayes told southern Democratic leaders he would end **12)** _____ if they would support him as President. Shortly after, he took office. Hayes had all federal **13)** _____ removed from the South.

Southern state governments denied African Americans social **14)** _____ and the right to vote. In many cases, **15)** _____ for African Americans were not much better than they had been before the Civil War.

Do You Remember?

Directions: Write the answers to these questions using
complete sentences.

1) What two companies were chosen to build the transcontinental railroad?

_____

_____

_____

2) What form of transportation did most Americans use to travel to the West before the completion of the transcontinental railroad?

_____

_____

_____

3) What improved communication in 1861?

_____

_____

_____

4) Before the transcontinental railroad was completed, how were goods and supplies shipped from east to west?

_____

_____

_____

5) How was the completion of the transcontinental railroad observed?

_____

_____

_____

Miners, Cowhands, and Farmers

Directions: Write each of the following words or phrases from the
Word Bank under the heading to which it belongs.

Word Bank		
branding	longhorns	silver strike
Chisholm Trail	Nevada	sod house
dry farming	Pikes Peak	stampede
gold strike	prospectors	Texas
homesteaders	railroad holding pens	windmills

Miners

_____

_____

_____

_____

_____

_____

Cowhands

_____

_____

_____

_____

_____

_____

Farmers

_____

_____

_____

_____

_____

_____

Plains Indians Crossword

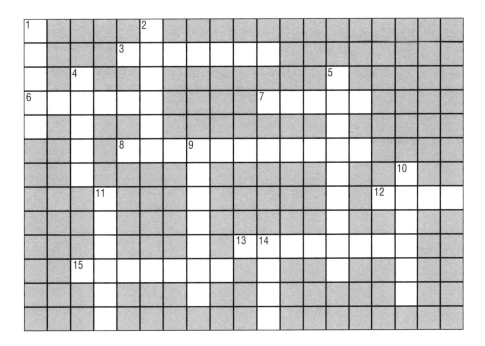

Across

3) One man killed 4,000 of these in eighteen months

6) American Indians believed the Great _____ lived in the Black Hills

7) Chief Red _____

8) People looking for gold

12) "Buffalo Bill"

13) One group that fought the Seventh Cavalry

15) State where battle occurred in June of 1876

Down

1) Chief Crazy _____

2) Man who led the Seventh Cavalry

4) The Black Hills were holy to these people

5) To give up to the enemy

9) Chief _____ Bull

10) Famous Nez Percé Chief

11) Territory where Black Hills were located

14) Little Big _____ River

Failed Attempts to Help American Indians

Directions: Choose a phrase from the box to complete each sentence
below. Write the correct answer on the line after
each question.

• no frontier line	• family-sized farms	• by government agents
• the vast western lands	• religious movement	• become farmers
• had been mistreated	• protect them from bullets	• killed or wounded
• every member of Congress		

1) *A Century of Dishonor* detailed how badly American Indians

_____

2) Helen Hunt Jackson's book was given to

_____

3) The Dawes Act was intended to help American Indians

_____

4) American Indian lands were divided into

_____

5) Sometimes, American Indians were victimized

_____

6) The Ghost Dance was a

_____

7) Some American Indians believed the Ghost Dance would

_____

8) At Wounded Knee, 290 Ghost Dance followers were

_____

9) By 1890, there was

_____

10) Between 1864 and 1912, thirteen states were created from

_____

Do You Remember?

Directions: Write the answers to these questions using
complete sentences.

1) What are some natural resources that contributed to America's industrial growth?

_____

_____

_____

2) How is iron purified to make steel?

_____

_____

_____

3) Why is steel a better construction material than iron?

_____

_____

_____

4) What is the Brooklyn Bridge?

_____

_____

_____

5) Who created the symbols for the two major political parties? What are those symbols?

_____

_____

_____

Major Industries

Directions: Match each item in Column A with a detail in Column
B. Write the letter of each correct answer on the line.

Column A

_____ **1)** Elisha Otis

_____ **2)** Horatio Alger

_____ **3)** Henry Ford

_____ **4)** Thomas Edison

_____ **5)** Booker T. Washington

_____ **6)** Nelson Morris

_____ **7)** Alexander Graham Bell

_____ **8)** New York Central

_____ **9)** George Washington Carver

_____ **10)** Cornelius Vanderbilt

_____ **11)** Great Northern

_____ **12)** George Eastman

_____ **13)** Ottmar Mergenthaler

_____ **14)** Menlo Park

_____ **15)** James J. Hill

Column B

a) invented early telephone

b) started Tuskegee Institute

c) location of Edison's research lab

d) invented the elevator

e) invented typesetting machine

f) "The Empire Builder"

g) scientist who aided farming

h) helped inspire child labor laws

i) invented indoor electric lightbulb

j) invented auto assembly line

k) worked on the camera

l) linked railroads in the Northeast

m) rail system to the Northwest

n) helped develop meat-packing industry

o) America's first great rail system

Do You Remember?

Directions: Write the answers to these questions using
complete sentences.

1) In 1850, what percentage of the U.S. population lived in cities?

_____

_____

_____

2) Where were factories usually built?

_____

_____

_____

3) What lowered the cost of products?

_____

_____

_____

4) During this period, how many hours a week did some factory employees work?

_____

_____

_____

5) Why was it not necessary for employers to pay high wages to factory workers?

_____

_____

_____

Immigrant Crossword

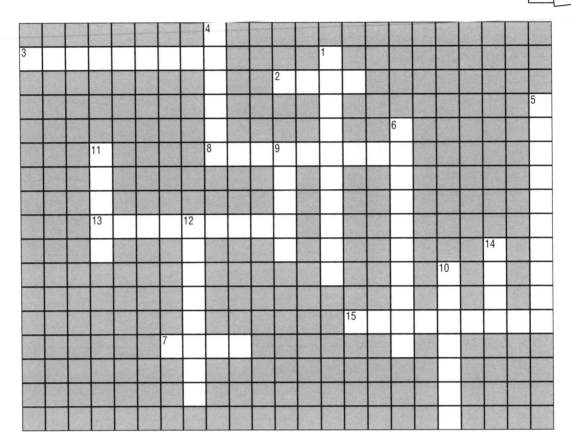

Across

2) Jim ___ Laws separated African Americans and whites

3) Action or belief against someone due to race, sex, religion, or age

7) Only the Supreme Court could reverse Jim Crow ___

8) Act passed in 1862 that offered farm land to immigrants

13) This state passed a law requiring "separate but equal" rail facilities

15) Some _____ did not like the new immigrants

Down

1) Amendment that applied to states and not individuals

4) Half of those who came from Poland and Russia were these people

5) Getting to America was difficult for most _____

6) Announced publicly

9) "Separate but _____"

10) In 1882, a new law said no more of these people could come to America

11) Country from which the largest group of "new immigrants" came

12) Part of a ship for passengers paying the lowest fare

14) Immigrants from this continent settled on the west coast

City Living

Directions: Complete the paragraphs below. Choose the correct term from the Word Bank.

Word Bank		
basketball	leisure	schedule
department	museums	specialized
electric	Naismith	spectator
fixed	orchestras	streetcars
income	retail	trolleys

American cities offered their residents theaters, music halls, skating rinks, and other
1) _____ activities. Libraries offered the opportunity to read books, while
2) _____ areas included different stores and restaurants.

City transportation included horse-drawn 3) _____ that carried ten to fifteen
people at a time. After Thomas Edison invented the 4) _____ motor, people traveled
in larger vehicles known as 5) _____ . These were usually inexpensive to ride, and
they ran on a set time 6) _____ .

The early stores 7) _____ in only a few products. Shoppers went from one
store to another. When business owners put many different stores into one large building, the
8) _____ stores became very popular. F. W. Woolworth was one of the first to offer
many different products at a 9) _____ price. People who live on a limited
10) _____ were able to purchase many items for a reasonable amount of money.

Many cities built opera houses and halls for symphony 11) _____ . Works of
art could be seen at public 12) _____ . Sports teams were organized in numerous
cities. Baseball became a favorite 13) _____ sport. James 14) _____
invented a new game known as 15) _____ .

City Problems

Directions: Read each statement. Choose the best meaning from the
Word Bank for the underlined word or phrase below.
Write the meaning in the space provided.

Word Bank	
city	tenements
dumbbell tenements	ventilation
immigrants	waste disposal
slums	Young Men's Christian Association
talents	Young Women's Christian Association

1) With the large numbers of people in many cities, <u>sanitation</u> was poor. _____

2) Hundreds of <u>five- or six-story buildings</u> were built in some areas. _____

3) The <u>YMCA</u> helped the urban poor. _____

4) As many as thirty-two families lived in <u>five- or six-story brick buildings</u>.

    _____

5) The <u>YWCA</u> also helped the urban poor. _____

6) Jacob Riis wrote about the living conditions of <u>people who had moved from other countries</u>.

    _____

7) Too many people had to live in <u>areas with poor living conditions</u>. _____

8) Some of the buildings had little <u>circulating fresh air</u> in them. _____

9) Some people believed that the poor were lazy or had no <u>skills</u>. _____

10) <u>Urban</u> leaders were not sure how to deal with many of the problems. _____

Do You Remember?

Directions: Write the answers to these questions using
complete sentences.

1) Why did Mark Twain use the term "Gilded Age" as a label for the 1870s?

_____

_____

_____

2) What feeling did reform leaders have about the industrial leaders?

_____

_____

_____

3) How did the Crédit Mobilier's activities affect its stock?

_____

_____

_____

4) What corrupt move did William Belknap make?

_____

_____

_____

5) What happened in the Whiskey Ring Scandal?

_____

_____

_____

Labor Unions

Directions: Complete the paragraphs below. Choose the correct
term from the Word Bank. You may use words more
than once.

Word Bank	
700,000	membership
all	Samuel Gompers
American Federation of Labor	secret
Chicago	strike
eight-hour	strikebreakers
Haymarket Square	Terence Powderly
Knights of Labor	workers

In 1869, Uriah Stephens organized the **1)** _____ . The union was small. It was
also a **2)** _____ organization. Ten years later a new leader named
3) _____ changed the union. The union accepted **4)** _____
workers. The membership grew to over **5)** _____ members.

Later, another union was formed. This union was called the **6)** _____ .
The union's leader was **7)** _____ . This new union organized many different skilled
8) _____ into one powerful union.

The most effective tool that the unions used to force businesses to meet their demands
was a **9)** _____ . Union workers refused to work for a company until their demands
were met. Companies sometimes hired workers to replace those who refused to work. These
nonunion workers were called **10)** _____ . Sometimes, violence would occur when
nonunion workers tried to take the jobs of union workers. One instance of violence was the
11) _____ bombing in the city of **12)** _____ . City workers were
on strike to gain an **13)** _____ workday. At a protest meeting, a bomb was thrown.
Several people were killed. This event hurt the movement. Many people blamed the
14) _____ for the people who were killed. After this event, the union's
15) _____ steadily declined.

The Populist Party

Directions: The words or phrases in the box refer to something that
was believed to help either big business or the average
American in the 1880s. Write each item under the
correct heading at the bottom of the page.

- gold standard
- graduated income tax
- higher farm prices
- President Cleveland
- James Weaver
- limited money supply
- Populist party
- Interstate Commerce Commission
- William McKinley
- William Jennings Bryan
- trusts
- silver coins
- Sherman Anti-Trust Act
- senators chosen by the people
- publicly owned railroad companies

Big Business

_____

_____

_____

_____

_____

_____

_____

_____

Average American

_____

_____

_____

_____

_____

_____

_____

_____

Do You Remember?

Directions: Write the answers to these questions using
complete sentences.

1) What helped put America in a better position to compete with the countries of Europe?

_____

_____

_____

2) What parts of the former Spanish empire remained in North America?

_____

_____

3) Why was America so concerned about Cuba?

_____

_____

_____

4) What did President McKinley offer to do in order to avoid a war with Spain?

_____

_____

_____

5) Why did Theodore Roosevelt send an American fleet to the Philippines?

_____

_____

_____

Splendid Little War

Directions: The statements below could have been made about
Cuba or the Philippines. Write each statement under the
correct heading at the bottom. Some statements may
apply to both countries.

- Admiral Dewey destroyed the Spanish navy there.

- The Rough Riders captured San Juan Hill there.

- In 1902, the United States made an agreement with
  this new republic.

- The United States paid Spain $20 million for it.

- It is in the Pacific Ocean.

- Its people wanted their own government.

- Walter Reed rid it of yellow fever.

- America could keep military bases there.

- American forces remained there for four years.

- The United States sent an army to stop its
  independence movement.

Cuba

_____

_____

_____

_____

_____

_____

_____

_____

_____

Philippines

_____

_____

_____

_____

_____

_____

_____

_____

_____

The United States and China

Directions: Match each item in Column A with a detail in Column
B. Write the letter of each correct answer on the line.

Column A

_____ **1)** foreigners

_____ **2)** Open Door Policy

_____ **3)** Hawaiian Islands

_____ **4)** John Hay

_____ **5)** Japan

_____ **6)** American universities

_____ **7)** European countries

_____ **8)** Boxers

_____ **9)** China's trade

_____ **10)** Pacific

_____ **11)** troops

_____ **12)** Boxer Rebellion

_____ **13)** Great Britain

_____ **14)** Chinese

_____ **15)** Philippines

Column B

a) U.S. Secretary of State

b) owned land in China

c) Chinese who rebelled

d) trading plan for China

e) ocean between China and United States

f) some Chinese wanted them out

g) Asian country that gained Chinese land

h) threatened to destroy Open Door Policy

i) money returned was used to send
Chinese young people to these

j) established own government and courts
in China

k) with Hawaii gave America a stronger
ability to trade with the Far East

l) became American territory in 1900

m) American merchants were afraid it would
fall under control of a few countries

n) sent to China to protect American
interests

o) revolt in China

Turn-of-the-Century Crossword

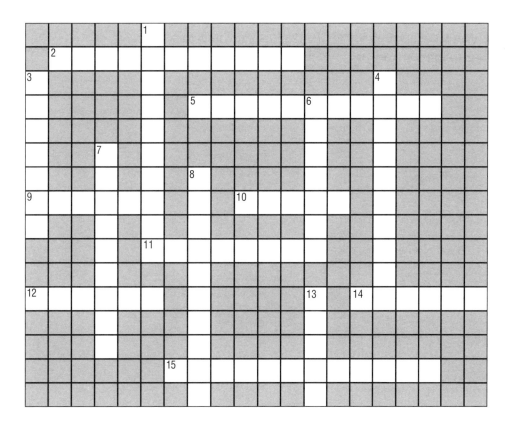

Across

2) Ida Tarbell accused him of making an oil monopoly

5) America set up a naval base here

9) Throughout the world

10) Democratic candidate in 1900

11) He was assassinated in 1901

12) Roosevelt agreed with striking coal _____

14) Vote out of office

15) New reform group

Down

1) The right voters have to approve or reject bills

3) Anti-Trust Act named for him

4) Power citizens have to suggest new laws

6) An election in which people choose the candidates

7) Took office in 1901

8) People who write about corruption

13) President Roosevelt became known as a "_____ buster"

Roosevelt Numbers

Directions: Choose a number from the box for each blank in the
sentences below. Write that number on the correct
blank. Some numbers may be used more than once.

3	1902	1908
10	1905	1914
150	1906	7,000

1) The Panama Canal was completed in _____ .

2) Roosevelt helped Russia and Japan end their war
   in _____ .

3) Congress passed the Meat Inspection Act in _____ .

4) Gifford Pinchot convinced the President to add
   _____ million acres of land to the country's
   forest preserve.

5) The federal government gained the power to build dams to
   create irrigation projects by a law passed in _____ .

6) Many state governments had set up their own conservation
   projects by the year _____ .

7) The United States had _____ foreign policy plans.

8) The Republic of Panama received $ _____ million
   from the United States, plus yearly rent.

9) The Panama Canal took _____ years to build.

10) The Panama Canal cut the distance from New York to San
    Francisco by more than _____ miles.

Roosevelt Becomes a Bull Moose

Directions: Complete the paragraphs below. Choose the correct term or phrase from the Word Bank.

Word Bank

American Tobacco Company	Republican party
Bull Moose party	Robert E. Peary
Congress	Sixteenth Amendment
Democratic party	Standard Oil Trust
Department of Labor	William Howard Taft
Matthew Henson	William Jennings Bryan
New Freedom	Woodrow Wilson
New Nationalism	

President Roosevelt, not wanting a third term in office, convinced the
1) _____ to nominate 2) _____ . Their candidate had no trouble winning the presidency. He defeated the
3) _____ candidate, 4) _____ .

President Taft took office in 1909. That same year, two men discovered the North Pole. African American 5) _____ accompanied
6) _____ on that journey as well as many others during a twenty-year period.

President Taft demanded a restructuring of the 7) _____ and he ordered the break-up of the 8) _____ . During his administration, 9) _____ gave the government power to collect income taxes, through the passage of the 10) _____ . Also, the
11) _____ was set up.

In 1912, Roosevelt sought re-election as a candidate of the
12) _____ . This candidate went against Republican Taft and the Democratic candidate, 13) _____ . The Democrats promised a program called the 14) _____ , while Roosevelt called his plan the
15) _____ . The Democrats won the election.

Do You Remember?

Directions: Write the answers to these questions using
complete sentences.

1) What political experience did Woodrow Wilson have before he became President?

_____

_____

_____

2) What specific event started the war?

_____

_____

_____

3) Explain the chain reaction that occurred when Austria-Hungary declared war on Serbia.

_____

_____

_____

4) Which countries made up the Central Powers?

_____

_____

_____

5) Which countries made up the Allied Powers?

_____

_____

_____

The United States Stays Neutral

Directions: Fill in the blanks in each sentence with either *America,*
Great Britain, Germany, or *France.* Write the name of the
correct country on each line.

1) Although _____ wanted to remain neutral, it carried
supplies across the Atlantic Ocean.

2) _____ accused _____ of not
remaining neutral.

3) America provided goods to _____
and _____ .

4) Meanwhile, _____ tried to prevent America from
trading with _____ .

5) _____ set up a war zone around _____ .

6) The Allied Powers seemed to be losing to the Central Powers, so
_____ became concerned about the future
of _____ .

7) America felt a loyalty to _____ , because that country
had been an ally during the Revolutionary War.

8) Many Americans began to feel that _____ was cruel.

9) The *Lusitania*, while traveling from _____ to
_____ , was destroyed by a U-boat
from _____ .

10) The people of _____ wanted to declare war
on _____ .

World War I Crossword

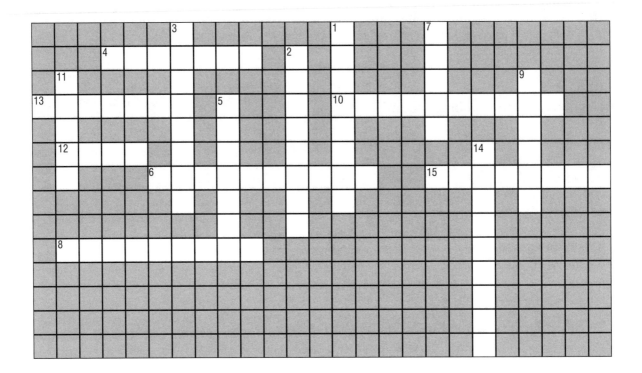

Across

4) President Wilson wanted America to fight for "peace and _____"

6) German note to Mexico

8) American soldiers were called "_____"

10) Something not changing or improving

12) Americans limited use of this to allow more for the military

13) One of the states Germany said it would give Mexico

15) Day, hour, and month that the war ended

Down

1) General whose men upset the German stronghold

2) American factories stopped production of _____ goods to make war supplies

3) Ocean in which U-boats caused so much damage

5) Officers from this country met Allied officers in a railroad car in France

7) The government sold these to raise money for the war

9) Germany asked these for an armistice

11) Practice of requiring people to serve in the armed forces

14) The _____ Service added men to the military

The League of Nations

Directions: Match each item in Column A with a detail in Column B. Write the letter of each correct answer on the line.

Column A

_____ 1) Versailles

_____ 2) Germany

_____ 3) President Wilson

_____ 4) Austro-Hungarian Empire

_____ 5) Asia and Africa

_____ 6) David Lloyd George

_____ 7) Poland

_____ 8) Paris

_____ 9) Georges Clemenceau

_____ 10) United States

_____ 11) Bosnia and Serbia

_____ 12) Czechoslovakia

_____ 13) Republican senators

_____ 14) Vittorio Orlando

_____ 15) The U.S. Senate

Column B

a) did not join League of Nations

b) became part of Yugoslavia

c) one country given land after war

d) representative of Great Britain

e) palace where peace conference met

f) one new nation created after war

g) did not like the Treaty of Versailles

h) blamed for starting the war

i) carried his message to the people by train

j) split into Austria and Hungary

k) representative of Italy

l) city near which world leaders met

m) twice voted against the Treaty
of Versailles

n) representative of France

o) former German colonies were here

Do You Remember?

Directions: Write the answers to these questions using
complete sentences.

1) Who led the National Woman Suffrage Association?

_____

_____

_____

2) What percentage of the popular vote did Warren Harding receive in the election of 1920?

_____

_____

_____

3) What event led to Calvin Coolidge becoming President?

_____

_____

_____

4) Why was the Veteran's Bureau established?

_____

_____

_____

5) Secretary of the Interior Albert B. Fall was jailed because of his role in what political scandal?

_____

_____

_____

Society Changes

Directions: Choose the phrase from the Word Bank that will best
complete the sentences below. Write a phrase on
each line.

Word Bank

assembly line	Communication by phone	older generation
became affordable	fastest speed	social changes
challenge old ideas	leisure time	social freedom
changed gears	monthly payments	ten million Americans
commercial radio station	more mobile	unlimited source

1) Many _____ occurred in America in the 1920s.

2) People's purchasing power changed with a new ability to buy things in _____ .

3) _____ helped to bring people closer together.

4) Americans had more money and more _____ .

5) As more people bought cars, the society became _____ .

6) In the mid-1920s, the price of cars dropped, so they _____ to a greater
number of Americans.

7) The Model T was the first car made on an _____ .

8) Unlike our modern cars, the early automobiles were able to travel a _____ of
forty miles per hour.

9) When driving the Model T, Americans _____ by using a foot pedal.

10) Women of the 1920s refused to be tied down to the actions of the _____ .

11) Women began to _____ about how they should act.

12) Women's desire to gain more _____ could be seen in the changes in their
style of dressing.

13) The radio became an _____ of free information and entertainment.

14) In 1920, the first _____ began broadcasting in Pittsburgh.

15) By 1929, about _____ owned radios.

Social Problems

Directions: Each statement below is related to the Immigration Act, the Ku Klux Klan, or Prohibition. Write each statement under the correct heading at the bottom of the page.

- The Twenty-First Amendment repealed it.
- Its people helped elect governors in two states.
- New people from Japan were not allowed in America.
- It limited the number of immigrants from Europe.
- Because of this, the 1920s became known as "The Dry Decade."
- It was formed in the South.
- Because of it, speakeasies became popular.
- It came into being in 1924.
- Its people held a parade in Washington.
- It was brought about by the Eighteenth Amendment.

Immigration Act

_____

_____

_____

_____

Ku Klux Klan

_____

_____

_____

_____

Prohibition

_____

_____

_____

_____

American Confidence

Directions: Match each item in Column A with a detail in Column B. Write the letter of each correct answer on the line.

Column A

_____ **1)** Herbert Hoover

_____ **2)** Great Depression

_____ **3)** United States

_____ **4)** Charles Lindbergh

_____ **5)** Al Smith

_____ **6)** stock market

_____ **7)** profit

_____ **8)** *Spirit of St. Louis*

_____ **9)** soup houses

_____ **10)** Radio Corporation of America

_____ **11)** Babe Ruth

_____ **12)** Calvin Coolidge

_____ **13)** Paris, France

_____ **14)** New York

_____ **15)** Roaring Twenties

Column B

a) man who made first solo flight

b) he hit sixty home runs

c) its stock rose by over $400 a share in one year

d) Lindbergh's destination

e) Republican nominee in 1928

f) he did not seek re-election in 1928

g) city Lindbergh left from

h) Hoover's opponent in 1928

i) what stock buyers hoped to make

j) Great Depression was the worst depression in its history

k) name for a decade

l) Republican campaign posters said Smith would bring on these

m) name of Lindbergh's plane

n) market for buying and selling stock

o) a time of great struggle

Do You Remember?

Directions: Write the answers to these questions using
complete sentences.

1) How did Americans lose confidence?

_____

_____

_____

2) How had businesses grown during the 1920s?

_____

_____

_____

3) What were two reasons for the decline in American exports during the 1920s?

_____

_____

_____

4) Why was industrial production slowed after 1930?

_____

_____

_____

5) Why did many banks go out of business during the depression?

_____

_____

_____

Hoover or Roosevelt?

Directions: The plans in the box were suggested by either Herbert
Hoover or Franklin Roosevelt. Write each one under the
correct heading at the bottom.

- The Tennessee Valley Authority put thousands to work on construction projects.

- A moratorium was put on war debts to the United States in hope that Europe would be better able to buy American products.

- The National Recovery Administration was established to help businesses recover.

- The Federal Emergency Relief Administration loaned money to states for food, clothing, and shelter for the poor.

- The Emergency Banking Act made federal loans available to banks.

- Congress approved $500 million to buy surplus crops from farmers.

- A federal public works program was set up to spend $750 million on jobs.

- The Reconstruction Finance Corporation was established to lend money to banks, insurance companies, and railroads.

- A national "bank holiday" was set up to prevent people from taking out all of their money from banks.

- The Civilian Conservation Corps hired young people to plant trees, work on roads, and help with rural flood control.

Herbert Hoover

_____

_____

_____

_____

Franklin Roosevelt

_____

_____

_____

_____

New Deal Crossword

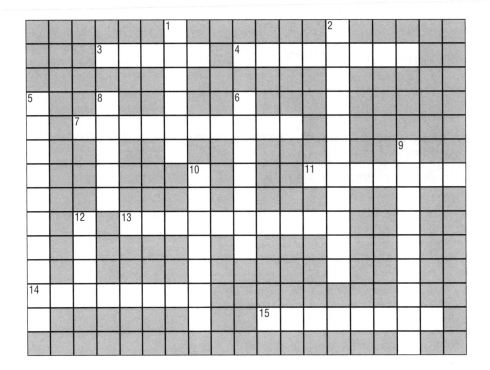

Across

3) Painting or drawing on a wall

4) Social _____ Act

7) Type of bargaining between workers and employers

11) African Americans had voted Republican because of him

13) Person's job or line of work

14) To reverse

15) To reject or show disapproval

Down

1) Other name for the National Labor Relations Act

2) The usual way of doing things

5) American _____ of Labor

6) One who favors change

8) _____ Progress Administration

9) New Deal programs helped restore the _____

10) Federal _____ Administration

12) Number of "old men" Roosevelt saw in Supreme Court

Depression Leisure and Literature

Directions: Match each item in Column A with a detail in Column
B. Write the letter of each correct answer on the line.

Column A

_____ **1)** Ginger Rogers

_____ **2)** *The Wizard of Oz*

_____ **3)** Federal Communications
Commission

_____ **4)** Fred Astaire

_____ **5)** Max Schmeling

_____ **6)** Adolf Hitler

_____ **7)** Jesse Owens

_____ **8)** Shirley Temple

_____ **9)** Scarlett O'Hara

_____ **10)** Margaret Mitchell

_____ **11)** Orson Welles

_____ **12)** Wallace Carothers

_____ **13)** Amelia Earhart

_____ **14)** Joe Louis

_____ **15)** Marx Brothers

Column B

a) crazy comedians

b) spun first man-made fibers

c) wrote *Gone With the Wind*

d) female dance partner

e) first woman to fly Pacific Ocean solo

f) produced *The War of the Worlds*

g) world heavyweight champion

h) male dance partner

i) American Olympic runner

j) German boxer

k) child star

l) investigated and passed regulations

m) German leader

n) character in *Gone With the Wind*

o) popular film of the 1930s

Do You Remember?

Directions: Write the answers to these questions using
complete sentences.

1) What was a major factor in the collapse of the German economy in 1923?

_____

_____

_____

2) What group of people were stripped of their citizenship and property by the Nazis?

_____

_____

_____

3) What was Adolf Hitler's title? What did it mean?

_____

_____

_____

4) Why did Americans feel safe from foreign attack?

_____

_____

_____

5) What did the neutrality laws of 1935 and 1937 forbid?

_____

_____

_____

The Beginning of the War

Directions: During the early years of World War II, the following
statements might have been made by certain world
leaders. After each statement, write *C* for Winston
Churchill, *H* for Adolf Hitler, *R* for Franklin Roosevelt,
or *S* for Joseph Stalin.

1) "Poland surrendered a few weeks after we attacked it."
_____

2) "We must rescue the soldiers at Dunkirk." _____

3) "I shall insist that the RAF increase its defenses." _____

4) "We should consider lending arms to France and Great Britain."
_____

5) "Hitler can't be trusted. We must now join the others, for this
man wants to conquer Europe." _____

6) "Our island must defend itself at any cost." _____

7) "I believe this policy will keep us out of the war." _____

8) "Gentlemen, I ask you to approve these funds to ready us
for war." _____

9) "Tell them we will grant them rights to our naval bases."
_____

10) "What? Is he forgetting our friendship treaty?" _____

11) "Our troops and troops from France and Belgium were trapped
at the sea." _____

12) "We will stage a blitzkrieg." _____

13) "We must come to the aid of Poland." _____

14) "Like it or not, we'll have to begin a lottery for more soldiers."
_____

15) "Using their bases, we can protect the Panama Canal."
_____

War in Asia

Directions: Complete the paragraphs below. Choose the correct term from the Word Bank.

Word Bank		
alliance	Filipino troops	lend-lease
allies	gained control	naval fleet
announcement	gaining	negotiate
battleships	infamy	oil
empire	lack of	victory

America's Open Door Policy was threatened by the **1)** _____ of Japan that it intended to rule all of Asia, including China. Japan continued its plan to create an **2)** _____ . It went on to form an **3)** _____ with Germany and Italy.

After Japan conquered Indochina, America became concerned that Japan was **4)** _____ too much land. In response, the United states stopped selling steel and **5)** _____ to that country. In the meantime, America offered a **6)** _____ plan to China. Japan's Premier Fumimaro Konoye and Secretary of State Cordell Hull began to **7)** _____ .

On December 7, 1941, 353 Japanese airplanes set off to destroy the American **8)** _____ at Pearl Harbor. Within hours, the American Pacific fleet had lost many **9)** _____ , destroyers, and planes. More than 2,000 Americans had been killed. President Roosevelt referred to December 7 as a "date that will live on in **10)** _____ ." Japan's **11)** _____ , Germany and Italy, soon declared war on the United States.

In the Philippines, American and **12)** _____ fought the Japanese. Because the Filipinos and Americans had a **13)** _____ vehicles and ammunition, Japan had gained another **14)** _____ . Japan had **15)** _____ of the Philippines.

The Home Front

Directions: Match each item in Column A with a detail in Column B. Write the letter of each correct answer on the line.

Column A

_____ **1)** volunteers

_____ **2)** industries

_____ **3)** General Motors

_____ **4)** civilians

_____ **5)** bacon grease

_____ **6)** underestimated

_____ **7)** shortages

_____ **8)** combat

_____ **9)** pressure of war

_____ **10)** victory gardens

_____ **11)** gunpowder bags

_____ **12)** detention

_____ **13)** many Japanese Americans

_____ **14)** ration

_____ **15)** posters

Column B

a) caused nation to set aside democratic principles

b) to use sparingly

c) to fail to guess size, quantity, or number

d) worn stockings were used to make these

e) fighting

f) needed raw materials

g) parks and flower beds were turned into these gardens

h) holding someone against his or her will

i) changed styles of women's clothes

j) was able to make more war supplies than all of Germany and Japan

k) fought bravely in Europe

l) reminded Americans of their duty

m) collected tires, cans, and papers

n) used for making ammunition

o) people who are not in military

The War Ends

Directions: The statements in the box are about the final days of
World War II. However, they are in the wrong order.
Rewrite them on the lines at the bottom, in the order in
which they occurred.

- President Roosevelt died.

- Allied leaders met in Yalta.

- President Roosevelt was re-elected.

- The United States dropped an atomic bomb on Nagasaki.

- General MacArthur accepted the surrender of Japan.

- The United States dropped an atomic bomb on Hiroshima.

- President Truman gave a last warning to Japan.

- Germany surrendered.

- The Allies began an invasion of Japan.

- The Soviet Union entered the war against Japan.

---

1) _____

2) _____

3) _____

4) _____

5) _____

6) _____

7) _____

8) _____

9) _____

10) _____

Do You Remember?

Directions: Write the answers to these questions using
complete sentences.

1) How many American men and women did the United States lose in World War II?

_____

_____

_____

2) What five nations were made permanent members of the United Nations Security Council in 1945?

_____

_____

_____

3) What were the four features of President Truman's "Fair Deal?"

_____

_____

_____

4) What did the Taft-Hartley Act prevent employers from doing?

_____

_____

_____

5) Who was the Republican party's nominee for President in 1948?

_____

_____

_____

Cold War Crossword

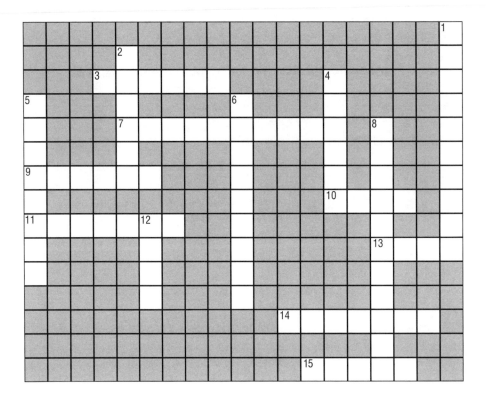

Across

3) Doctrine of containment was named for him

7) First head of the NATO force

9) After the war, the United States began a struggle with the _____ Union

10) Many countries formed this alliance in 1949

11) Using planes to deliver food and supplies

13) Churchill said that an "_____ curtain had descended"

14) To lower upon

15) Agreement signed at the end of World War II

Down

1) Complete control

2) Nation that had serious political and economic problems and a civil war after World War II

4) German city that was closed off

5) Secretary of State

6) He challenged the United States to contain communism

8) Policy of using force to control spread of communism

12) Number of divisions in Germany after the war

Korean War

Directions: Complete the paragraphs below. Choose the correct
term from the Word Bank. Some may be used more
than once.

Word Bank	
China	Republic of Korea
communists	Seoul
Democratic People's Republic	Soviet Union
General Douglas MacArthur	United Nations
Manchuria	United Nations Security Council
President Truman	United States
Pusan	

After World War II, Korea was divided into two parts. The northern section was held by
the **1)** _____ , while the south was controlled by the **2)** _____ . America
withdrew its troops when the **3)** _____ was set up, but North Korea remained
the **4)** _____ .

After North Korea invaded the south, the **5)** _____ announced that the
move was wrong. South Korea asked the **6)** _____ for its help. Because they had been
boycotting that organization, the **7)** _____ was unable to veto the plan of action.
8) _____ sent American troops to help South Korea.

North Korea captured the South Korean capital of **9)** _____ .
10) _____ set up a defensive line of American troops at the port of
11) _____ . He and his troops were able to push the North Korean army toward the
Chinese province of **12)** _____ .

13) _____ asked President Truman for permission to bomb
14) _____ . When Truman refused, he went to Congress. As a result, Truman
fired him.

Peace talks began in July of 1951. Both the north and the south withdrew from their battle
line. The North Koreans and Chinese who opposed the **15)** _____ were able to remain
in South Korea.

Challenge in the 1950s

Directions: Match each item in Column A with a detail in Column B. Write the letter of each correct answer on the line.

Column A

_____ 1) Korean War veterans

_____ 2) Rosa Parks

_____ 3) Earl Warren

_____ 4) Martin Luther King Jr.

_____ 5) National Guard

_____ 6) technology

_____ 7) bomb shelters

_____ 8) Dwight D. Eisenhower

_____ 9) *Sputnik*

_____ 10) Joseph McCarthy

_____ 11) Republicans

_____ 12) Howdy Doody

_____ 13) Thurgood Marshall

_____ 14) nuclear war

_____ 15) Adlai Stevenson

Column B

a) senator who used fear of communism for his political gains

b) defeated in 1952

c) a new threat to Americans

d) stressed the need for change

e) were buying new homes

f) NAACP lawyer

g) Supreme Court Chief Justice

h) was called into Little Rock

i) advances in it offered a better life

j) television puppet

k) minister who led bus boycott

l) Soviet satellite

m) elected in 1952

n) woman who challenged segregation

o) were built in many backyards

Do You Remember?

Directions: Write the answers to these questions using
complete sentences.

1) What does NASA stand for?

_____

_____

_____

2) Why didn't Eisenhower run for re-election in 1960?

_____

_____

_____

3) Who was the Republican candidate in the 1960 election? What political experience did this
man have?

_____

_____

_____

4) What role did television play in the 1960 presidential election?

_____

_____

_____

5) There were two things about President Kennedy that made him a unique President. What
were they?

_____

_____

_____

Supporting Freedom Abroad

Directions: The statements below may have been made by world leaders during the early 1960s. Write *JK* if you think John Kennedy may have said it, *NK* for Nikita Khrushchev, and *FC* for Fidel Castro.

1) "It is time to force them out of West Berlin." _____

2) "I just received a letter from the Premier." _____

3) "The United States will not leave Berlin." _____

4) "I am telling you we need your help." _____

5) "I feel he is too young and inexperienced." _____

6) "I will authorize the training, but no other participation."
_____

7) "We have killed or captured most of the invaders." _____

8) "I don't care if it belongs to Americans. Seize it!" _____

9) "We will build a wall down the middle." _____

10) "I led the revolt against our dictator." _____

11) "You must give me your word that you will not invade Cuba."
_____

12) "I take full responsibility for the failed Bay of Pigs invasion."
_____

13) "The navy must stop those ships." _____

14) "I order our ships to return at once." _____

15) "We have discovered that Cuba has hidden missiles." _____

Struggles at Home and Abroad

Directions: Write the correct word from the Word Bank to complete each sentence.

Word Bank	
federal government	Tonkin Gulf
Great Society	President Kennedy
Medicare	Urban
Paris, France	Vietcong
Poverty	Vietnam

1) President Johnson challenged America to wage a "War on _____ ."

2) During the 1964 presidential campaign, Johnson challenged the people to make America a "_____ ."

3) Johnson's opponent, Senator Barry Goldwater, felt that the _____ should not interfere in states' policies.

4) Johnson's _____ plan provided health insurance for the elderly.

5) Robert Weaver was appointed head of the new Department of Housing and _____ development.

6) Johnson decided to expand America's role in an Asian country called South _____ .

7) _____ had sent only military advisors to Vietnam.

8) The Congressional vote on the right to "take all necessary measures" to protect American forces was called the _____ Resolution.

9) As _____ groups were destroyed, they were replenished by North Vietnamese.

10) In 1969, a meeting among North and South Vietnam, the United States, and the Vietcong was held in _____ .

New Movements in America

Directions: Match each item in Column A with a detail in Column
B. Write the letter of each correct answer on the line.

Column A

_____ 1) Malcolm X

_____ 2) Equal Rights Amendment

_____ 3) Altamont

_____ 4) Stokely Carmichael

_____ 5) Nobel Peace Prize

_____ 6) baby boom

_____ 7) AIM

_____ 8) War in Vietnam

_____ 9) hippies

_____ 10) college students

_____ 11) Woodstock

_____ 12) Black Power

_____ 13) counterculture

_____ 14) feminists

_____ 15) Cesar Chavez

Column B

a) rock music became its voice

b) New York rock concert

c) extreme members of the youth culture

d) wanted more control over studies

e) Black Muslim leader

f) wanted more African-American power

g) fought for women's rights

h) movement that promoted African-
American heritage

i) it was passed by many states

j) subject of much protest

k) led Mexican-American migrants

l) set up for American Indians

m) those born right after World War II

n) music festival where someone died

o) awarded to Martin Luther King Jr.

Politics of Protest

Directions: The statements in the box might have been said about
American political figures during the 1960s. Write each
statement under the correct heading at the bottom of
the page.

- He was elected President in 1968.

- On June 6, 1968, he died.

- His convention was very confused.

- His promise was an end to the Vietnam War.

- His campaign for President had been gaining strength.

- He wanted to "Bring Us Together."

- Many felt he would follow Johnson's policies.

- This man died in Memphis.

- He tried to please both sides in the Vietnam disagreements.

- In a speech, he referred to the "Promised Land."

Robert Kennedy

_____

_____

Martin Luther King Jr.

_____

_____

Lyndon Johnson

_____

Hubert Humphrey

_____

_____

Richard Nixon

_____

_____

Do You Remember?

Directions: Write the answers to these questions using
complete sentences.

1) Which astronaut was the first to walk on the moon? On what date?

_____

_____

_____

2) Who ran for President against Richard Nixon in 1972?

_____

_____

_____

3) What did the War Powers Act require?

_____

_____

_____

4) At what university did National Guardsmen fire at student protesters?

_____

_____

_____

5) How many Americans were killed in Vietnam? How much did the war cost?

_____

_____

_____

Nixon's Foreign Relations

Directions: Match each item in Column A with a detail in Column B. Write the letter of each correct answer on the line.

Column A

_____ **1)** Henry Kissinger

_____ **2)** SALT

_____ **3)** Cold War

_____ **4)** People's Republic

_____ **5)** Brezhnev

_____ **6)** détente

_____ **7)** Taiwan

_____ **8)** Pacific

_____ **9)** China

_____ **10)** President Nixon

_____ **11)** Chou En-lai

_____ **12)** space exploration

_____ **13)** rivals

_____ **14)** American people

_____ **15)** Moscow

Column B

a) Soviet President

b) one of America's enemies in the Korean War

c) Nixon's top foreign policy adviser

d) neither the United States or China would dominate it

e) Soviet city that Nixon visited

f) hoped to improve relations with the Chinese and Soviets

g) Americans and Soviets agreed to cooperate on this

h) what China and the Soviet Union were becoming

i) was shocked that Nixon would visit China

j) name for communist China

k) French word for "relaxation"

l) the United States had called this the legal government of China

m) Nixon wanted to relax its tensions

n) arms limitation treaty

o) Chinese Premier

More Struggles at Home Crossword

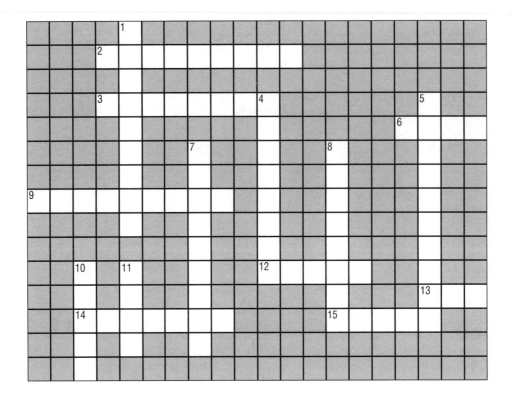

Across

2) Nixon said some of his were wrong

3) What burglars placed on phones

6) Became President in 1974

9) Building that housed Democratic main office

12) People who assist

13) Special prosecutor

14) Failing to pay one's taxes is tax _____

15) FBI agent who wanted to spy on Democrats

Down

1) The House _____ Committee had grounds for impeachment

4) A court order

5) Joint act of breaking the law

7) Stealing money by using some kind of threat

8) Chairman of CREEP

10) Committee for Nixon's re-election

11) One of Nixon's aides who was fired

Ford Administration

Directions: Complete the paragraphs below. Choose the correct term or phrase from the Word Bank.

Word Bank	
bicentennial	pardoning
criticized	Queen Elizabeth of Great Britain
embargo	sailing ships
Exporting	shocked
gas stations	United States
heating oil	*Viking I*
Israel	Watergate
Mars	

Shortly after becoming President, Gerald Ford surprised the nation by
1) _____ Richard Nixon. Although President Ford felt the nation needed to forget
2) _____ , he was **3)** _____ for this action.

During a conflict between Arab states and **4)** _____ , the Arab countries placed
an **5)** _____ on oil shipments to many countries, including the United States.
Americans had to wait in long lines at **6)** _____ and there was a shortage of home
7) _____ . Americans were **8)** _____ at how dependent they were on other
countries. The Organization of Petroleum **9)** _____ Countries began to regulate oil
prices. This drove up the price of gasoline and heating oil in the **10)** _____ .

On July 4, 1976, America celebrated the **11)** _____ of its Declaration of
Independence. **12)** _____ presented America with a six-ton bell.
More than 200 large **13)** _____ came from thirty nations. Two weeks after the
celebration, the spaceship **14)** _____ successfully landed on **15)** _____ .

A New Leader

Directions: The statements in the box could have been made about different countries of the world in the 1970s. Write each statement under the correct heading below.

- Arab neighbors refused to recognize its right to exist.
- Anwar Sadat was its president.
- Civil war broke out here.
- Israel bombed it several times.
- It finally recognized Israel as an independent state in 1979.
- Its dictator, Anastasio Somoza, was overthrown.
- Many PLO members were located here.
- Menachem Begin was its prime minister.
- Was not happy that America owned the Panama Canal.
- Will gain control of the Panama Canal in 2000.

Egypt

_____

_____

Israel

_____

_____

Lebanon

_____

_____

Nicaragua

_____

_____

Panama

_____

_____

International Problems

Directions: Each statement below could have been made about a
country in the 1970s. Decide which country each
statement applies to. Write *US* for United States, *IR* for
Iran, *SU* for the Soviet Union, or *AF* for Afghanistan
after each statement.

1) Eight American soldiers died on its desert. _____

2) Iranian students here organized protests. _____

3) Sixty-six people from this country were taken hostage.
_____

4) Babrak Karmal was its new president. _____

5) Its president and his family were executed. _____

6) Its president ordered all oil imports stopped. _____

7) The United States stopped sending wheat to this country.
_____

8) They claimed the United States stole money from them.
_____

9) Its former leader came to the United States for medical
treatment. _____

10) Kabul is its capital. _____

11) The United States boycotted the Olympics here. _____

12) It refused to return the Shah to his homeland. _____

13) Its president, as of 1979, was the Ayatollah Khomeini. _____

14) The Soviets invaded it. _____

15) Its leader signed SALT II with President Carter. _____

Do You Remember?

Directions: Write the answers to these questions using complete sentences.

1) What happened to the fifty-two American hostages in Iran on the day President Reagan took office?

_____

_____

_____

2) Why is Mount St. Helens about 1,300 feet shorter than it was before 1980?

_____

_____

_____

3) What bill, passed at the urging of President Reagan, provided tax and spending cuts?

_____

_____

_____

4) How did Justice O'Connor believe the Supreme Court should interpret the Constitution?

_____

_____

_____

5) How long had the space shuttle *Challenger* been in the air before it exploded?

_____

_____

_____

International Issues Crossword

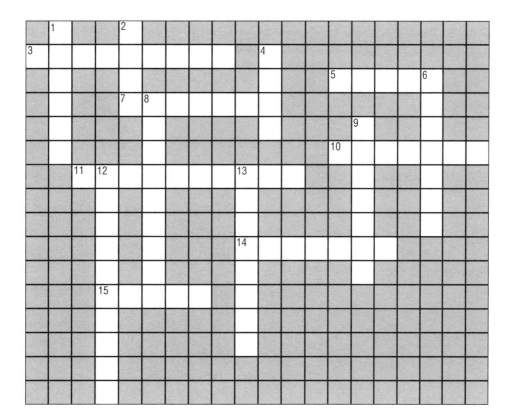

Across

3) Communist government took power in this Central American country in 1979

5) The _____ government of South Africa denied equal rights to black people

7) Muammar al-_____ was the Libyan leader

10) Country where 200 American soldiers died at Marine base

11) Libyan _____ killed Americans in Rome and Vienna

14) Nicaraguan rebels

15) President of Egypt

Down

1) President Reagan froze all _____ assets in America

2) Country that fired missile at *U.S.S. Stark*

4) Reagan called the Soviet Union the "_____ Empire"

6) Reagan didn't want to do too much damage to the South African _____

8) Separation of white ruling class and black people in South Africa

9) Gulf where United States began to protect oil tankers

12) Devices such as bombs

13) Action taken to force a country to do something

A New President

Directions: Match each item in Column A with a detail in Column
B. Write the letter of each correct answer on the line.

Column A

_____ **1)** deficit

_____ **2)** Douglas Wilder

_____ **3)** Colin Powell

_____ **4)** Soviet Union

_____ **5)** drug abuse

_____ **6)** Cold War

_____ **7)** Deficit Reduction Plan

_____ **8)** polls

_____ **9)** David Dinkins

_____ **10)** East Germany

_____ **11)** Jesse Jackson

_____ **12)** Hungary

_____ **13)** George Bush

_____ **14)** Michael Dukakis

_____ **15)** Berlin Wall

Column B

a) 1988 Republican presidential candidate

b) are used to guess election outcomes

c) its government announced citizens were free to
leave

d) 1988 Democratic presidential candidate

e) spending more than what is taken in

f) African-American mayor of New York City

g) President Bush said it would end when Europe
was "whole"

h) began to protest communist rule

i) had been having economic problems

j) Chairman of the Joint Chiefs of Staff

k) President Bush called it a "scourge"

l) African-American governor of Virginia

m) German city's divider

n) it would increase taxes and limit spending

o) African-American candidate for President

Do You Remember?

Directions: Write the answers to these questions using complete sentences.

1) What three former Soviet republics were the first to join the Commonwealth of Independent States?

_____

_____

_____

2) The Soviet Union controlled many eastern European countries through a trade association. What was the name of that association?

_____

_____

_____

3) Which countries saw themselves as winners of the Cold War?

_____

_____

_____

4) How did the Internet begin?

_____

_____

_____

5) Name three countries that had been under Soviet control that declared their independence by the early 1990s.

_____

_____

_____

Gulf War Crossword

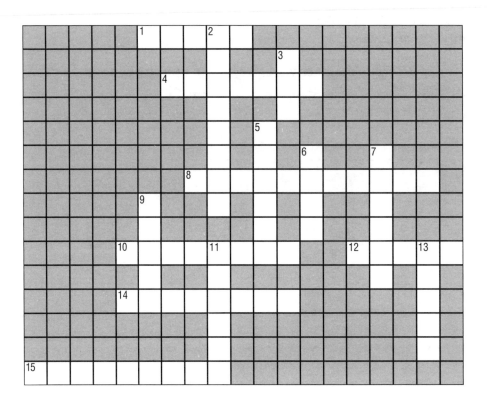

Across

1) "Operation Desert Shield" became
    "Operation Desert _____"

4) Iraqi leader

8) Commander of the Allied forces in Kuwait

10) Person wounded, killed, or missing
    in action

12) Allied planes rained _____ on Iraq and
    Iraqi forces in Kuwait

14) When this passed, the United States would
    attack the Iraqi army

15) Those skilled at negotiating
    among nations

Down

2) Countries worried about one nation
    having so much control over an important
    natural _____

3) Persian Gulf nations agreed to raise the
    price on it

5) Country Iraq invaded

6) During the war, _____ and western
    nations cooperated

7) Iraq was their _____ enemy

9) President Bush wanted to bring a lasting
    _____ to the Middle East

11) Those who fought Iraq

13) Secretary of State

The Clinton Administration

Directions: Match each item in Column A with a detail in Column
B. Write the letter of each correct answer on the line.

Column A

_____ 1) James Brady

_____ 2) conservatives

_____ 3) First Lady Hillary
Rodham Clinton

_____ 4) Congress

_____ 5) Omnibus

_____ 6) Dan Quayle

_____ 7) alliances

_____ 8) huge tariffs

_____ 9) Ross Perot

_____ 10) Theodore Roosevelt

_____ 11) Arkansas

_____ 12) $496 million

_____ 13) Democrats

_____ 14) NAFTA

_____ 15) Carol-Mosely Braun

Column B

a) trade agreement among United States, Mexico, and Canada

b) African-American senator from Illinois

c) bill named for him called for a national computer network to check gun buyers

d) third-party candidate who had strong showing at the polls in 1912

e) they kept control of Congress

f) budget cut total over five years

g) rejected health care plan

h) argued that budget bill relied on high taxes and too few cuts

i) Violent Crime Control and Prevention Act

j) state from which President Clinton came

k) groups of health care professionals

l) third-party candidate with strong showing in 1992

m) Mexico would end these under NAFTA

n) Republican vice presidential candidate in 1992

o) helped create health care plan

Foreign Issues

Directions: The statements in the box could have been made about
different countries of the world during the 1990s. Write
each statement under the correct heading at the bottom
of the page.

> • Its leader, Jean-Bertrand Aristide, was removed from office.
>
> • UN troops went there with food in 1993.
>
> • President Clinton hosted a summit with this country and the PLO.
>
> • American casualties forced withdrawal of troops in 1994.
>
> • Former President Carter was sent there to negotiate with rebels.
>
> • The United States promised to protect it in case of war.
>
> • In 1994, it signed a peace treaty ending a forty-six-year war.
>
> • It was part of the former Yugoslavia.
>
> • It agreed to take down its nuclear arsenal.

Israel

_____

_____

Somalia

_____

_____

Russia and the Ukraine

_____

_____

Bosnia-Herzegovina

_____

Haiti

_____

_____

Problems and Changes

Directions: Write the word or phrase from the Word Bank that best completes each sentence.

Word Bank	
balanced	nineteen children
church buildings	second term
Contract	shutdowns
impeachment	upon the states
minimum wage bill	World Trade Center

1) In 1994, a Republican plan called the "_____ With America" was introduced.

2) One bill that called for a _____ federal budget by the year 2002 was passed by the House but rejected by the Senate.

3) The disagreements between the President and members of Congress resulted in some temporary government _____ .

4) In 1993, a bomb exploded in the parking garage of the _____ in New York.

5) A car bomb exploded near the Federal Building in Oklahoma City, killing 169 people, including _____ .

6) A welfare reform bill, passed in 1995, placed more responsibility for dealing with poverty _____ .

7) The Emergency Management Agency was ordered to help make _____ in the South more secure from arson fires.

8) President Clinton believed that a _____ would enable workers to raise stronger families.

9) Clinton was the first Democratic President to be elected to a _____ since Franklin D. Roosevelt.

10) In 1998, the House of Representatives voted two articles of _____, but the Senate acquitted President Clinton.

The Year 2000 Crossword

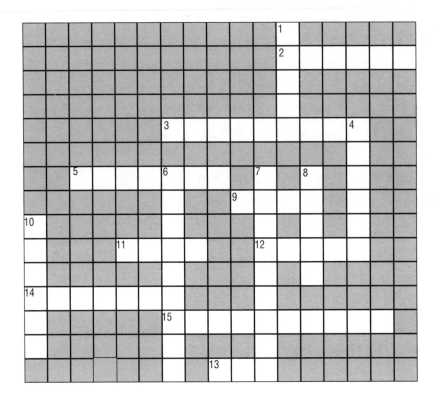

Across

2) Pat Buchanan's party

3) largest number of immigrants in 2000

5) campaign issue about the budget

9) Democratic presidential candidate

11) Third World countries have this

12) a hope for the twenty-first century

13) people worried about the rising price of this

14) people fear a proliferation of this type of warfare

15) 1,000 years

Down

1) Ralph Nader's party

4) the part of Congress that holds impeachment trials

6) Al Gore's running mate

7) people feared the Y2K Bug in these

8) George W. Bush was governor of this state

10) where the 2000 Summer Olympics were held